The Public Library of Nashville and Davidson County

Religious Right, Religious Wrong

Lloyd J. Averill

Foreword by Martin E. Marty

The Pilgrim Press
NEW YORK

Copyright © 1989 The Pilgrim Press
All rights reserved

Biblical quotations are from the Revised Standard Version of the Bible, copyright 1946, 1952 and 1971, 1973 by Division of Christian Education, National Council of Churches, and are used by permission.

Library of Congress Cataloging-in-Publication Data

Averill, Lloyd J. (Lloyd James), 1923–
    Religious right, religious wrong.

    Bibliography: p. 183
    1. Fundamentalism—Controversial literature.
I. Title.
BT82.2.A85   1989   230'.044   88–32097
ISBN 0-8298-0804-3

The Pilgrim Press, 132 West 31st Street, New York, N.Y. 10001

This book is dedicated to my grandchildren
Kellen and Stacy Averill
Berit and Aaron Graham
Shannon, Cameron, Christopher,
and Kathryn Taylor
with faith, hope, and love

Contents

Foreword

Fundamentalism. The subject is on page one and part of primetime news coverage. It is a major force around the world, one which caught most non-Fundamentalists off guard. Fundamentalists, be they Christian, Islamic, Jewish, or anything else, were on guard and are not surprised by this current surge. They believe that history is in God's hands, that they are God's agents, and that in God's good time their hour for action comes.

Non-Fundamentalists, on the other hand, particularly in our Western world, traditionally saw Fundamentalism as a relic, a kind of spiritual set of dinosaur bones which belonged in a museum. The tide of history was against Fundamentalisms. History was on the side of reason, science, and progress. Every time one looked, she might expect to find less religion than the time before. Every time one assessed religion, he would find it more rational, scientific, and progressive.

This, at least, was what people thought in the first quarter of this century, when Fundamentalism was taking shape, acquiring a name, and getting ready for battles with moderates, liberals, and modernists in Protestant denominations. Beaten back, Fundamentalists seemed to slink away, to live on in hillbilly, backcountry, holyrolling, redneck territories. Wherever they were, however, they built Bible colleges, radio networks, new denominations, new images. By midcentury they were back, in moderate, scrubbed-up, neo-evan-

gelical forms, in the mode of Billy Graham. That flank of
Fundamentalist-born believers moved ever closer to the
mainstream, however one defines that.

In the fourth quarter of the century, in the period of the
nation's bicentennial and the election of evangelical Jimmy
Carter, and then through the years of Ronald Reagan's presidency, tougher-minded, hard-lining Fundamentalism was
back. By now it understood and used the new technology of
television and computers. This Fundamentalism produced
celebrities who crowded mainstream and evangelical Protestants off the front (and sometimes back) pages of news-
papers. It had an aggressive agenda and was ready to assert
itself in politics.

Now, late in this fourth quarter, Lloyd J. Averill reviews
the century's game so far and looks at the prospects near its
end. I can best serve the reader by describing his book's tone,
genre, and place. Here is my attempt.

Long before Averill, Fundamentalist bashing was the thing
to do. Secular and religious non-Fundamentalists always
found in it an ogre, a bogey, a fossil, over against which to
define themselves. Just prior to Averill, Fundamentalist chic
was in. Neoconservatives in culture, people with long mem-
ories who were full of resentment at the modernism that
prevailed in 1925 and the liberal secular theology of 1965,
could not quite bring themselves to defend Fundamentalism. But in an "at-least-by-God-they-believe-something"
spirit they used its presence to bash moderates and liberals.
Many moderates and liberals seemed masochistically to enjoy being bashed and withheld criticism and set out to ride
out the storm.

There were, of course, some counteractors. One group,
People for the American Way, was successful in blocking
Fundamentalist moves in politics. Some secular commentators asked, "Where is the church in all this?" Why was
there not a single well-known Protestant or Catholic theologian or leader up front protecting civil liberties, liberal positions, theological openness, and a spirit of tolerance? The
answer could have been, "There probably were, but they did
not raise their voices enough to be heard"; or, "It took them a

while to get their act together, since they had dismissed Fundamentalism so long ago."

Now that the bashing days and the time of chic sympathy are gone, Lloyd Averill is free to bring a new synthetic perspective. His subtitle says that this is a critique, and it is. He believes that Fundamentalism is ultimately a distortion of the message of God, the ways of Christ, the possible connections with the world, and the best of hopes for the future. And he tells why he believes that in important pages in this book. But his sixth chapter shows that he can temper criticism with empathy, can speak of "religious wrong" and still take lessons from the "religious right."

With this book Professor Averill enters his own mature definitions and assessments, is ready to argue eloquently for them and shows that he is ready to keep on learning. But, more important, he is setting out to help non-Fundamentalist believers and non-religious bystanders understand what is going on. So the secular critics who had and have been asking, "Where are the rest of you Christians when we need a critique?" have their answer. Here, at least speaking for many, is an informed voice. And I would hope that Fundamentalists would read this and say, without being able to agree with the author, that he has understood them, presented them fairly, and helped continue and improve a conversation which will remain vital for years to come.

So this is an important book, broad in its sweep and yet ready to go deep where necessary. It would provide a good manual for discussion in congregations or classrooms, but it is equally valuable for the lonely searcher who wants to make sense of a world that is changing so rapidly, is full of threat and, on occasion, shows promise. Averill's book is a signal of promise.

MARTIN E. MARTY

Preface

THIS BOOK HAS BEEN WRITTEN with the specific concerns and questions of certain readers very much in mind:

- "mainstream" Christians, both Protestant and Roman Catholic, who are puzzled by fundamentalism and especially troubled by its claim of exclusive rights to the Christian name but who are not sure what kind of religious response can be made to that claim

- persons who have made their way out of the fundamentalist movement, who still feel the residual pull of its absolutist demands and the personal pain of their separation, and who want—indeed, who need—some reassurance that there are legitimate Christian grounds for rejecting those demands and some redeeming Christian purpose for enduring that pain

- secularists whose intellectual curiosity leads them to wonder what the shouting is all about or who are alarmed by the intensity of fundamentalism's apparent singlemindedness and its political ambition and who wonder what its real prospects are

- "mainstream" Christians, ex-fundamentalists, and secularists who find it difficult to believe that there are, in the fundamentalist movement, any redeeming qualities whatever.

During earlier decades of this century, fundamentalism was an ignorable phenomenon on the fringes of American public life. It was discredited and obscured from public view by its anti-intellectualism (before 1960 there was scarcely a standard publishing house in the country that would touch a fundamentalist manuscript). It was dismissed because of its reputation for intramural contentiousness and brawling. And it was given an Elmer Gantry image, or at least tagged as bizarre, by the behavior of some of its more notorious head-liners, such as the flamboyant California evangelist Aimee Semple McPherson; the Texas Baptist Frank Norris, who once shot a man to death in his church study; and the baseball-player-turned-tent-evangelist Billy Sunday.

Two things, among others, altered fundamentalism's public persona in recent years. One was a turn to the right in American politics, most sharply during the Reagan years. The public attractiveness and new credibility enjoyed by rightist politics gave credibility to rightist religion; and, in turn, rightist religion gave sanction, not to say sanctification, to rightist politics. It was a marriage literally made in heaven, in the view of its political and religious enthusiasts.

The other factor that altered the public status of funda-mentalism, chronologically coincident with the first, was also a combined secular and religious development. Televi-sion increasingly replaced radio as the primary means of popular communication, displaying a capacity for social influence unknown in radio days. Fundamentalists in search of an enlarged public gained increasing mastery of the new medium, as once they had exploited radio, but with a signifi-cant difference: they were now able to fuse entertainment with religion (consider all of the fundamentalist clones of "The Tonight Show") in a way radio never permitted and to command an increasing audience drawn as much for the former as for the latter.

Fundamentalism is thus a phenomenon to be reckoned with, now as never before in this century. *How* it may be reckoned is the subject of this book. Lest any prospective reader be misled, let me make it clear from the outset that I consider fundamentalism, in many though not all of its features, to be a faith turned in upon itself and consequently ungenerous and unlovely in its religion, flawed in its under-standing of history, and dangerous in its politics. Since I intend to be critical of the movement, I accept the obligation to describe it as accurately as I can, since nothing is to be gained from the criticism of a phantom or fantasy. And because I believe that there are some important redeeming characteristics in the movement that deserve acknowledgment along with its more specious features, I intend in a concluding chapter to make that acknowledgment as appreciatively as I can.

LLOYD J. AVERILL

Acknowledgments

THIS MATERIAL ORIGINALLY was presented as a series of lectures entitled "The Religious Right: What Is It Up To?" given at the Richmond Beach Congregational Church in Seattle, at the urging of its pastor, Stephen Hanning, and with the cosponsorship of the Northwest Theological Union. The series was subsequently repeated at St. Barnabas Episcopal Church, Bainbridge Island, Washington; Lord of Life Lutheran Church, Renton, Washington; and the Seattle First Baptist Church. Individual lectures from the series were given at Plymouth Congregational Church and St. Andrew's Episcopal Church, both in Seattle; to the Bishops and Church Executives group of the Church Council of Greater Seattle; at the University of Washington School of Social Work; and in the "Target UW" series on issues of nuclear war, sponsored by a university student group.

To all of those organizations, to the individuals who issued the invitations, and especially to those who attended, listened, and responded, I express my appreciation.

Certain persons have been particularly helpful in their encouragement to translate the lectures into book form. Chief among them is my wife, Carol White. Others include Ginger and Lyn Walker, Katharine and Scott Briar, Katie and Duane Pasco, Marty and Bill Holm, and Barry Herem, all of whom have my affectionate gratitude.

Some of my earlier work predisposed, and in important ways shaped, this present work. Three articles in The Chris-

tian Century probed the fundamentalist phenomenon. "Political Fundamentalism in Profile" (12 August 1964) was subsequently reprinted by The Christian Century Foundation for quantity distribution during the 1964 presidential campaign and appeared still later in substantially revised form as "Political Fundamentalists and Other Reactionaries: The Escape from Freedom" in my book, *The Problems of Being Human* (1974). "Can Evangelicalism Survive in the Context of Free Inquiry?" (22 October 1975) tested the claim of certain Christian institutions of higher education to be universities in the full classical meaning of that term. And a 19 January 1983 article entitled "Is the End Near?" has been expanded into chapter 5 of the present work. The editors of *The Christian Century* have my thanks for permission to reshape some of that material for the purpose of this book.

Some reflections of my *American Theology in the Liberal Tradition* (1967) are to be found in chapter 2, "Fundamentalist Beginnings: Saying No to the Modern Era."

It is a pleasure to acknowledge other authors and editors from whom I have learned and whose work has enriched and enlarged my own. That acknowledgment is given fully in Appendix B, which appears at the conclusion of this volume.

Finally, I want to express my considerable appreciation to several others whose influence on this book has been direct and substantial: to Martin E. Marty for reading the manuscript and endorsing its publication; to an anonymous evangelical scholar, who also read the manuscript, enduring exasperation at a number of points in that reading, whose valuable and carefully annotated comments gave me an opportunity to reconsider, and in places to alter, what I had originally intended to say; to my wife, and to good friends Katie Pasco, M. Kent Mayfield, and Spencer C. Bennett, for their thoughtful reading of the manuscript and their supportive responses to it; and to my staff assistant, Linnea Little, for her careful and critical reading and her helpful suggestions based on a direct acquaintance with the movement that is the subject of these chapters.

While all of the persons named above have contributed significantly to the descriptions and analyses contained in this book, the final responsibility for its fairness and facticity is, of course, my own.

CHAPTER 1

The Right and the Left: Getting Our Directions Straight

A COUPLE OF YEARS AGO, my father, who was then eighty-six, wrote me a letter in which he said, "Can you tell me the difference between the right and the left?"

He wasn't unsure about the proper designation of his hands and feet, nor was he expressing a confusion brought on by advanced age. In my twice-monthly telephone conversations with him, I have yet to detect any such sign of his near-nonagenarian status. Nor did his question suggest a lack of reading or reflection. Until his eyes began to weaken, he had been an inveterate reader; and, though lacking a college education, he has always taken a thoughtful interest in the world around him.

His question about the meaning of the right and the left came, rather, from the uncertainty any of us might experience at any age, these days. Those terms are applied to a wide variety of phenomena, including politics, religion, the writing of history, the study of economics, and the creation of art. And their meaning in any one of those areas may or may not bear directly on their meaning in the others. Moreover, attributions of right or left are sometimes intended to convey pride or compliment, sometimes to unleash abuse or condemnation; and unless you can see an accompanying smile or snarl, it may not always be clear which is intended.

The whole scene becomes even more complicated when

we add terms like radical, **liberal**,* moderate, **conservative, evangelical, fundamentalist,** and reactionary, not to mention the confusion we may experience in having a politician, for example, identified as a moderate conservative or a moderate liberal. Historians speak of the left wing of the Reformation, meaning the Mennonites and other nonconformist groups that grew up in the fifteenth and sixteenth centuries in eastern and northern Europe. And while those groups were, and their contemporary successors are, radical in some of their religious and social views—they embody a tradition of pacifism, for example—they were and are conservative in others, especially in their efforts to resist materialism and to maintain a simplicity of life. So it would not be inappropriate to think of them as radical conservatives.

And in recent years, when commentators have taken to writing about the New Right and the New Left, one need not be an octogenarian to experience confusion.

ON BEING HUMAN

At bottom, what distinguishes left from right—what separates them on the ideological spectrum, whether in religion or in politics—is the difference in their views of what it is to be human. Each of them, taken at its extreme and in isolation from the other, is an act of dehumanization. Each by itself is an effort to flatten out the threatening ambiguities of our humanness. Each by itself is an effort to escape the tension and anxiety that come from living fully in the presence of both *freedom and fate,* which are the primary coordinates for locating human being in contrast to all other created forms of being. Taken at their extremes, in isolation from each other, left and right represent an effort to seize one of those two coordinates as if the other did not exist; as if the one alone told the real and full truth about our humanhood;

---

*A brief set of Key Terms is provided in Appendix A, as a supplement to explanations in the text and an aid to readers who may be unfamiliar with theological terminology. The first time a word appears that is defined in the Appendix, it is in boldface type.

as if we could live really and fully human lives unidimensionally.

Of course, that's an illusion, and we ought to say so plainly to the extremists. From the moment of conception, each of us inherits a past, a history, both biologically and culturally. At birth, each of us *is* a history—it is our prevenient humanness—until we begin to acquire our own distinctive past to add to that inherited history; and the two—the past inherited and the past lived—become an organic whole. They are what they are: unchangeable, irrevocable, inescapably our own. Together they constitute our fate.

Yet, true as that is—and it is an absolutely elemental fact of our humanness—it is nevertheless not the whole truth. There is another rock fact about us that fully matches fate in its significance; namely, that being human means being fated to be free. If we are not free to decide whether or not we shall have a past or which past we shall have, if we are not free to wish or wipe out of existence what is past, we are free to take up a position with respect to the past, to decide what attitude we shall take toward it, what we will make of it, in every present. If we cannot revoke the past at the level of event, we can rework it at the level of significance. The variety of ways in which we can interpret and reinterpret our past, in which we can recombine its elements and utilize it, the variety of ways in which we can value it and revalue it, are for all practical purposes inexhaustible. So, sometimes in defiance of our past and sometimes in conspiracy with it, we choose moment by moment what we shall make of ourselves and our world.

Omar Khayyám understood fate:

> The Moving Finger writes, and having writ,
> Moves on; nor all thy Piety nor Wit
>   Shall lure it back to cancel half a line,
> Nor all thy Tears wash out a Word of it.[1]

A character in Ellis Arnall's *The Shore Dimly Seen* understood freedom:

> "You know what I think? I think that everything you do today, or I do, affects not only what is going to happen but what

already has happened, years and centuries ago. Maybe you can't change what has passed, but you can change all the meaning of what has passed. You can even take all the meaning away. That is why we have to be careful."[2]

There is something frightening about fate, about the inescapability of my past. And there is something comforting in it, for its very irrevocable character seems to offer me a plausible denial of culpability. There is something exhilarating about freedom, promising me liberation from the drag of the past. And there is something frightening in it—Jean-Paul Sartre said we are "condemned" to be free—because it explodes the myth of plausible deniability, making me responsible not only for my future but for my past as well.

To be fully human is to live, ambiguously, at this troubling intersection of fate and freedom.

FREEDOM OR FATE

Neither the left nor the right understands this complex, anxiety-producing, and for that very reason creativity-generating, truth about our humanhood, and therefore it seeks to ignore or to suppress one or the other of its essential terms.

The left, at its extreme, seizes upon freedom as the whole truth. It is rooted in the assumption that the human ought not to be what it has been, but only what it will be; that to link a person, however tenuously, to a past is to distort and oppress; and that the nature of the human can be changed simply by reconceiving it and willing the reconception. The left absolutizes some future aspiration—some as-yet-unrealized set of values, some as-yet-unshaped institutions; it seeks to hold the present hostage to that dream and to force the future to fit its lineaments. It takes the view that history can be created *de novo*, beginning with the present moment; that we are free to shape history as if there were no past; that we need only claim the courage to set our own precedents without consulting any alleged wisdom that may have gone before us.

We saw these characteristics of the left at work in the

campus and urban activists of the late 1960s and early 1970s in this country. They believed that anyone older than thirty had been corrupted irreversibly by a corrupting society, and that only the young, who were relatively untainted by the social past, could be trusted to envision a radically new order and bring it into being. They actually believed that their own generation was, in fact, a new breed of humanity, free of the sins of their elders, able to see truth with clear eyes and, contrary to the self-deceptions of their parents, able to tell the truth "like it is." They repudiated established social structures, in the conviction that institutions are contrary to nature because they frustrate the uninhibited freedom that nature intended to confer upon every person. Institutions, in their view, compel one to give up doing "his own thing," forcing attention instead upon a corporate and therefore compromised will; all of which is to say that institutions rob their members of true individuality and real integrity. So, in the view of the New Left activists, the only way to recover true humanhood was to tear down all social institutions, in expectation that Eden would be restored thereby and innocence regained.

The irony of all this, an irony lost on large numbers of those activists at the time, given their intensity and single-mindedness, was that the instruments they chose to bring in their new order—intolerance, rhetorical excess, and acts of egregious violence—simply imitated the worst features of the old order they professed to detest.

We have also seen the characteristics of the left, configured somewhat differently but reflecting the same unidimensional view of human nature, in the Soviet Union, with its suppression of tradition represented by organized religion; its conviction that Soviet man is a new man, able by the principles of a "scientific" humanism to live without the myths and meanings of the past. It holds the doctrine that human nature is energized solely by economic interests, needs, and desires, to which all other motivations—spiritual, ethical, intellectual, aesthetic—are subordinated. It has a utopian confidence that a radically new order is under construction, a classless society from which the individual self-interest and greed that corrupt capitalism will be purged and replaced by rational economic planning and decision making. And it has the faith, evidence to the contrary notwithstanding, that the future is irrevocably on the side of the Marxist-Leninist philosophy.

One of the tragic miscalculations of the Communist left has been its failure to understand that revolutionary leaders, who are "temporarily" invested with absolute political authority in order to create the new society in a hurry—even when it is announced in advance that authority will be transferred to the people once social justice has been achieved—will become so enamored of their power that they will never voluntarily relinquish it and will invent whatever historical and ideological fictions may be necessary to hold on to it. So the "new man" of the Communist left turns out to live by the same law as the "old man" of the bourgeois capitalism it professes to detest: that "power corrupts" and that "absolute power corrupts absolutely."

The right, at its extreme, seizes upon fate as the whole truth about our humanhood. It is rooted in the assumption that the human ought to be only what it has been, and that any effort to alter that human condition is contrary to nature and to nature's God. The right absolutizes elements out of the past—some set of valued traditions, some idealized conditions, whether real or mythical, that shaped a "golden age," and the structures that sustained it. The right seeks to hold the present hostage to that nostalgia and to restrict and reshape the present to its procrustean image. It confers privileged status on some elite, whether derived from genetic fate, such as race, or from inheritance, such as aristocratic lineage or landed estate, or from faithful adherence to an orthodoxy drawn from an authoritative past that gives legitimation to efforts to govern the present by its authority. It takes the view that history must be restrained because all valid precedents have already been established, and that safety for individuals and for society requires disciplined conformity to the valued patterns of the past, in order to avoid the peril that may otherwise lie, waiting and subversive, in an uncontrolled future.

We have seen these characteristics of the right at work in the Union of South Africa. Its prevailing religious faith is a backward-looking, rigidly biblicist Dutch Calvinism, and its political faith rings the changes on an idealized past in which colonial dominance over indigenous people was virtually absolute. Its policy of apartheid is designed to perpetuate the political and economic privilege of the white minority, at the expense and the massive disadvantage of the nonwhite majority. It has stubbornly resisted even gradual change toward new social and political practices and institutions and has attempted to force conformity to the established order by repressive decrees that limit the freedom not alone of its nonwhite inhabitants but of its white citizenry as well.

We have also seen these characteristics, somewhat differently configured, in right-wing regimes in Portugal and Spain earlier in this century and in Latin America past and present. In these places, tradition-bound political practices were often formally allied with, and given respectability by, a backward-looking, rigidly dogmatic Roman Catholicism that prevailed in those countries prior to Vatican II. Political and economic power was the exclusive privilege of a reactionary coalition made up of the military, wealthy landowners, and religious leaders, who used arbitrary, harsh, and repressive measures to force a popular conformity to their collective will. Political legitimation derived not so much from positive programs as from official anti-Communism—resistance to the social and economic changes embodied in a Communist threat that was sometimes real, sometimes merely contrived to avoid any erosion of the privileges enjoyed by the power elite.

The left and the right have two things in common. One is that their beguiling attractiveness lies in a promise to relieve men and women of the lived ambiguity and anxiety of authentic humanhood and to replace it with the certainty and single-mindedness of a unidimensional existence, the left by effectively getting rid of fate, the right by effectively getting rid of freedom.

The other common attribute is that, at their extreme, they

cannot survive without coerciveness. However momentarily attractive it may be to be relieved of the burden of a fated existence, our human nature causes us to yearn for some organic connection with the past; and since such connection is subversive of the left, the left must force its adherents to do without it. However momentarily attractive it may be to be relieved of the burden of choice, with all decisions determined by the absolute authority of the past, our human nature causes us to yearn for the idiosyncratic, for a choice distinctly our own; and since idiosyncrasy is subversive of the right, the right must force its adherents to do without it.

So, although they occupy opposite sides of the ideological spectrum, and although each declares the other to be its mortal enemy, the irony is that, at their extreme, left and right are repressively undistinguishable.

FUNDAMENTALISM ON THE RIGHT

I have defined these positions at their extremes because it is easier to achieve reasonable clarity there. The fact is, of course, that the ideological scale is a continuum. From its center leftward there is increasing importance attached to freedom, less and less to fate, until at the extreme left freedom is all and fate virtually disappears. Similarly, from the center rightward there is increasing importance attached to fate, less and less to freedom, until at the extreme right fate is all and freedom virtually disappears.

This is a book about that party of the religious right, which is commonly designated by the term fundamentalism. Although it will anticipate somewhat the more detailed exposition and argument that follows, it may be useful in this prologue on ideological definition to show briefly how fundamentalism qualifies for denomination as a rightist movement, relatively far over toward its extreme. What may seem abstract in this brief, preliminary characterization will be made fully concrete in the main body of the book.

The legitimation claimed by fundamentalism, and indeed its entire agenda, is derived from the past; and although it projects a detailed, dramatic scenario onto the future, that expectation is drawn entirely from documents that are centuries old and alleged to contain that predetermined future in wholly reliable but encoded form. Fundamentalism takes its authorization from human encounters with the divine that occurred prior to the end of the first century A.D. and never occurred again with the same authority. Those encounters were recorded, preserved, and transmitted in a distinctive literature, the Bible, whose human authors merely wrote as God directed them. In the fundamentalist view, truth—whether about human personality, human society, or even the phenomena that are the stuff of the natural sciences—is not something that is progressively realized through the course of history as a result of painstaking human digging, imagining, sifting, and assessing; truth is, rather, something that was "once for all delivered" in the biblical record, so that the results of human investigation through time must be continually referred, for their validation, to that ancient norm. So fundamentalism asserts that history ought to be only what it has been, that present and future ought to be restricted and shaped to the procrustean record of the past. Thus, over time, fundamentalism has systematically resisted efforts to initiate change in social institutions, whether those changes have been in behalf of the civil rights of minorities, or of equal rights for women, or of family arrangements that differ from the traditional nuclear family, or of Constitutional interpretations that take into account conditions its signers could not have anticipated, or of the substitution of a newer world perspective for the old, narrow, chauvinistic nationalism. Typically, fundamentalists have charged that such changes are a departure from God's unchanging constitution for human life, a departure brought about by the active influence of Satan and his modernist allies. Fundamentalism insists on doctrinal conformity, enforced by an authoritarian leadership and reinforced by a spiritual coercion that threatens the pain of hell for any who dare to depart from the dogmatic norm. Those who, under conviction of sin, "give their hearts to Jesus" and are "born again" constitute an elite, whose spiritual and moral superiority presumably distinguishes them from all other sorts and conditions of humanity, including nonfundamentalist Christians, who are believed to be lost to God's plan of salvation because of the taint of doctrinal impurity.

VARIETIES OF FUNDAMENTALISM

Having used "fundamentalism" as a relatively undifferentiated term, both in this chapter and throughout the book, it is important both to acknowledge at the outset that the movement is far from monolithic—indeed, the point will be made later that it is inherently schismatic, which means that it exists in almost infinite variety—and at the same time to justify the use of that singular term.

First to the issue of variety. Fundamentalists differ in the matter of church organization. Some are found in congregations that are entirely independent, with no formal tie to any other congregation; some are gathered in formal denominations that nevertheless respect local congregational autonomy; and still others are gathered in denominations with a relatively high degree of hierarchical organization. One fundamentalist "association" was formed around the denial that organized denominations have any Christian validity, with no apparent sense of its own irony.

Not all fundamentalists are agreed on Christian baptism. Should it be administered to infants or only to adults? What should be its mode? Sprinkling? Immersion? Is it sufficient to immerse the candidate once, or must it be **trine immersion**, in which the candidate is lowered into the water three times in succession, once in the name of each Person of the Trinity?

Differences exist around the issue of the Lord's Supper. Should it be administered every Sunday or only on some less frequent schedule? Since the biblical account says that the original Last Supper occurred "when it was evening," should it now be administered exclusively at night? Who should be permitted to receive communion in a local church? Only those who have been immersed? Only those who have been baptized in that very congregation? Only those who have experienced trine immersion? Must commu-

nion be administered only in the presence of the congregation, or may it be administered individually, for
example to those who are house-bound?

Some fundamentalists believe that those who die in the
faith go at once to be with God in the full awareness of their
immortal beatitude; others believe in what is called "con-
ditional immortality," holding that the dead are unconscious
until the time of Christ's return to earth. Some believe Christ
will return before the great **tribulation** that will mark the end
of ordinary history, some that he will return in the midst of
that great struggle, and some that he will return at its conclusion. Some believe Christians are called to live a life of
self-denial; others that God intends to prosper with material
wealth those who love him. Some honor speaking in
tongues; some anathematize it. This account doesn't begin to
exhaust the varieties.

Yet, despite such differences, there are certain universals
that mark the variants as members of a common, if commonly contentious, family: together they trace their recent
historical origins to the **Evangelicalism** of the eighteenth
and nineteenth centuries; together they affirm the inerrancy
of scripture, and indeed, each uses biblical authority against
the others in defense of its own distinctive views; together
they expect the literal, **premillennial** return of Christ to
earth, sooner rather than later, however much they may
disagree on specifics of time and sequence; and together
they exhibit a common behavioral characteristic, separating
themselves religiously and prejudicially from those,
whether fundamentalists or others, from whom they differ
on doctrinal details. Paradoxically, such invidious *religious*
distinctions have not prevented them from coming together
around a common *political* agenda—one that includes
prayer and the teaching of creationism in the public schools;
control of local school boards by fundamentalist Christians;
opposition to abortion, to homosexual rights, and to equal
rights for women; and the importance of electing "born-
again" Christians to political office at every level, to name
only a few of its items.

These are the issues to which the chapters that follow are

devoted. These are the universals that make it legitimate to write about "fundamentalism" in univocal fashion, despite its intramural varieties.

INTERNAL CONFLICT

Anyone who undertakes to write about a strongly opinionated movement is likely to have strong opinions himself. In any event, there is no such thing as value-free inquiry. All investigation is done from the point of view of the inquirer, and deliberate efforts at objective statement are imperfect even under the best of circumstances. The least, and perhaps the most, I can do as an author is to let readers in on the presuppositions that inform my work, so that they can take account of my biases even when I fail to do so.

This book is both an exposition and a critique of the fundamentalist phenomenon, an effort to combine fair description with critical assessment. It is a critique because that phenomenon impresses me as spiritually and politically dangerous, for reasons to be adduced; it is an exposition because, unless viewed with clarity, any danger becomes more dangerous. My personal point of view, in fashioning both exposition and critique, is that of a Christian of evangelical liberal persuasion, which locates me somewhere left of center. The evangelical part means that, for me, faith subsists primarily in loyalty to the person of Jesus as the Christ—he who is himself good news, God's evangel. The liberal part means that no requirement may be placed on the life of faith that does not spring directly from that loyalty. Again, "evangelical" means beginning with the Bible at the points of its exclusive and authoritative witness to Jesus as the Christ; "liberal" means a conviction that God wants us to love him mindfully, not mindlessly, and a determination to use the best the contemporary culture has to offer in figuring out how to love God and be loyal to Jesus as the Christ in these times.

The historian Herbert Butterfield, late master of Peterhouse, Cambridge, who wrote about the origins of modern science and the relationship between Christianity and history, put what I take to be essentially the same view in terms that echo my earlier discussion of the tension between fate and freedom, and that effectively summarize the point of view from which I have written. Said Butterfield:

> There are times when we can never meet the future with sufficient elasticity of mind, especially if we are locked in the contemporary systems of thought. We can do worse than remember a principle which gives us a firm Rock and leaves us the maximum elasticity for our minds: the principle: Hold to Christ, and for the rest be totally uncommitted.[3]

CHAPTER 2

Fundamentalist Beginnings: Saying No to the Modern Era

THE FUNDAMENTALIST PHENOMENON first arose as a nine-teenth-century expression of theological alarm and historical disenchantment. Although the movement presented itself from the start as a return to the faith of the first apostles, it was, on the contrary, as new in its own way as the modernist theological formulations and the secularist social movements it found so threatening and denounced so virulently.

A CENTURY OF RAPID CHANGE

Looking back, we can see why the nineteenth century was no time for indifference. The pace of scientific, technological, social, and intellectual innovation was increasingly intense from the beginning of the century to its end on the eve of World War I, and that very intensity generated strong reactions, in some of enthusiasm and expectancy, in others of alienation and despair.

That perhaps unparalleled creative energy began, scientifically, with the publication in 1801 of Jean-Baptiste de Lamarck's theory of evolution, or "transformism" as he called it, an idea that was given even greater force fifty-eight years later by the appearance of Charles Darwin's *Origin of Species*. Seven years after Darwin's study appeared, the Austrian monk Gregor Mendel published the results of his breeding experiments with sweet peas, showing that inherited characteristics are determined by two hereditary units (now called genes), one from each of the parenting reproductive cells. Mendel's work was ignored in his own lifetime, but it was rediscovered in 1900 by three separate investigators and became the basis for the new science of genetics. It was in the same year, 1900, that Sigmund Freud published *The Interpretation of Dreams,* offering his first psychoanalytic model of mental functioning and setting in motion a revolution in understanding the dynamics of the human personality. In 1906, when the era was nearly over, Albert Einstein announced his "General Theory of Relativity," expanding the old three-dimensional universe to five dimensions and giving us a new understanding of space and time. However misplaced the application, this theory seemed, in the popular mind, to confer scientific respectability on notions of cultural relativism, especially in the spheres of religion and morals, thus creating a new problematic for subsequent generations to struggle with.

The combined influence of Lamarck, Darwin, Mendel, Freud, and Einstein has been enormous, disturbing old patterns of thought, leaving no department of the natural and social sciences untouched by their influence, and invading the most practical and intimate precincts of our lives ever since.

Technology made a somewhat slower start, but its achievements grew almost geometrically as the century progressed. Simply to list some of its most influential achievements is to sense the momentum of those times and the growing sense, then, that nothing on earth or in heaven was beyond mastery by human ingenuity, whether for good or ill. Here is an incomplete list of the century's inventions and medical advances, impressive in its very incompleteness: the opthalmoscope ,(1851), the rechargeable storage battery (1859), the typewriter (1867), antiseptic surgery (1867), the gasoline engine (1872), the microphone (1877), the incandescent lamp (1879), the linotype (1884), the steam turbine engine (1884), rabies vaccine (1885), aspirin (1889), the electric automobile (1892), tuberculin (1890), wireless telegraphy (1895), the diesel engine (1895), radioactivity (1896), experimental aircraft (1896), radium (1898), adrenalin (1901), the electrocardiograph (1903), the intelligence test (1905), the Wassermann test (1906), sulfanilamide theory (1908), vitamin A (1913), the x-ray tube (1913), and the radio transmitter (1914).

The effects of these developments on medical diagnosis and treatment, on communications and travel, and on living standards, especially in the West and more especially still in the United States, reached into the life of every person then and since.

Comparable influences of enormous potency were at work in the social movements of the nineteenth century. Feminism, so much a part of the present era, had its beginnings in a gathering in Seneca Falls, New York, in 1848, which issued the first public call for the electoral rights of women, a cause that grew under the leadership of Elizabeth Cady Stanton and Susan B. Anthony. The evils of the institution of slavery, and the rights and full humanity of those who had been enslaved, were championed in England by William Wilberforce, who secured parliamentary passage in 1807 of a bill abolishing the slave trade, and in the United States by William Lloyd Garrison, who founded the American Anti-Slavery Society in 1833; by Frederick Douglass, whose North Star newspaper advocated abolition through political action; and by Abraham Lincoln, whose Emancipation Proclamation was the fruit of this humanitarian heritage. Together these visionaries and activists inspired a popular revulsion against, and sparked organized efforts to eliminate, slavery around the world.

Under the influence of Samuel Gompers and others, the labor movement took shape in this country in 1886 with the founding of the American Federation of Labor, resulting, before the century was out, in higher wages, fewer working hours, and greater individual freedom for working men and women. The crusading journalist Jacob Riis, in the 1890s, called the attention of the nation to the appalling conditions of those who lived in urban slums. Riis founded a pioneer settlement house and gave impetus to the movement for playgrounds and public parks in American cities. In the work of Karl Marx, whose *Das Kapital* was published in three volumes between 1867 and 1894, those who had experienced the oppressiveness and the excesses of a crude capitalism were given a powerful instrument for ideological critique and an equally powerful intellectual center for organizing a competing economic and political movement—as it turned out, with scarcely less oppressiveness and excess. A new movement in support of conservation grew out of the presidency of Theodore Roosevelt (1901–1909), who ordered the first inventory of the country's natural resources and sponsored legislation to regulate and protect them. And the founding of the American nation and the adoption of its Constitution in 1789 inspired throughout the whole of the century that followed a demand for democratization that weakened the grip of arbitrary and hereditary regimes across the face of Europe.

All of that represents an astonishing record of social ferment, demanding a tolerance for change among nineteenth-century men and women rivaling any period in modern history. It would be understandable if some of them experienced psychic dizziness and disorientation.

And there is one more set of features, more intellectual than scientific or social, that must be added to this quickly drawn profile of a complex and provocative century, features that—even more directly than those described above—had a peculiar impact on the shaping of nineteenth-century religious dispositions.

In 1799 Friedrich Schleiermacher, perhaps the most influential theologian of the nineteenth century, published his first book, entitled *On Religion: Speeches to Its Cultured Despisers*, in which he argued that true religion is an affection, a feeling, an intuition, a "sense and taste for the Infinite." It is "the immediate consciousness of the universal existence of all finite things, in and through the Infinite, and of all temporal things in and through the Eternal." The effect of this experience of our primal unity with the whole of existence is an awareness of our absolute dependence on the

Ground of that unity, which is to say, an awareness of our absolute dependence on God. Some inevitable opaqueness results from stating so sophisticated an argument in such brief terms. The important thing is to understand what made Schleiermacher's formulation so radical: it cut nineteenth-century Christianity loose from dependence on the classical philosophical arguments for the existence of God, from dependence on creedal statements given authorization by sacred tradition, and even from dependence on a special **revelation** of God's character and intent in the biblical record. Instead, Schleiermacher urged that knowledge of the divine is to be found in the direct, immediate, conscious experience of every man and woman. The significance of Jesus Christ, on these terms, lies in "the constant potency of his God-consciousness," and Christ redeems us by calling us into fellowship and association with him, thus inducing in us an approach to his own immediate sense of God. Schleiermacher's emphasis on consciousness helped to shape a new discipline, the psychology of religion; and the idea of nurturing the God-consciousness gave later impetus to the religious education movement.

Albrecht Ritschl, another German theologian who was at work in the middle of the century, intended to correct Schleiermacher's view. Whereas the latter located God-awareness in a universal human consciousness, Ritschl found it in the historical figure of Jesus Christ, whose divinity lies in the fact that his "personal self-end has the same content as is contained in the self-end of God." Christ is God for us: we know God only in his direct influence upon us in the historical person of Christ. To be a believer, one must experience Christ in his own history. Unlike Schleiermacher, who placed exclusive emphasis on the religious consciousness, Ritschl insisted that the Christian faith is an ellipse with two foci: one is indeed religious, the redemption that is worked in us by Christ; and the other is ethical, namely, the kingdom of God, which Ritschl defined as "the moral organization of humanity through love-prompted action." The ultimate unity of these two, religious affection and ethical action, was demonstrated for Ritschl in the fact that "Christ made the universal moral Kingdom of God his end," and if we are Christians, we must do the same. Christ saves us, said Ritschl, by overcoming our sin and reproducing his own ethical faithfulness in us.

Ritschl's influence on the religious character of the era lay in his strong evocation of the historical person of Jesus Christ and in his insistence on the indispensability of Christian action in behalf of the kingdom of God.

The final element in this sketch comes out of nineteenth-century literary and linguistic studies of the classics and of German folklore. H. Gunkel and others concluded from those studies that behind ancient written documents—for example, the Old Testament—there is an even more ancient oral tradition; that material in the oral tradition passed through certain standard stages, or forms, which helped scholars to determine the relative age of material by the stage at which it had arrived; and that this developmental process was the product of the community rather than of an individual author. The final written form was often put together by an anonymous editor, who drew, sometimes critically and sometimes uncritically and at a considerable distance in time from the events described in the sources, from the combination of oral and written strands available to him. Gunkel also insisted that it is impossible to interpret a piece of ancient literature reliably without attempting to recover the historical life setting from which it drew breath, the occasion or occasions for which it was written, and its comparative relation to other literary products from the same historical and geographical location.

Two other literary scholars, J.H. Graf and Julius Wellhausen, developed what came to be known as the "documentary hypothesis" concerning the first five books of the Old Testament; namely, that these so-called Books of Moses are, in fact, composed of four distinct literary strands, each having its source in a different period and geographical location within the history of Israel, and were shaped in their present form by editorial hands long after Moses was dead.

The result of such literary criticism, applied to the Bible, was to call into question traditional claims for authorship (for example, that Moses wrote the Pentateuch) and hence to weaken the authority that authorship had been presumed to confer. Another result was to require a reconsideration of the dating of Old Testament books, usually by showing that they took their present form much later than had traditionally been thought. Still other consequences were to emphasize the human element in biblical formation and transmission and to require a thoroughgoing reconsideration of the overall authority of the Bible in the light of these new claims for its human character.

Clearly, the nineteenth century was a very busy, and for some a very unsettling, time.

THE MODERNIST RESPONSE

By no means everyone was unsettled by this astonishing rush of events. On the contrary, a large body of Protestant America welcomed it as a kind of revelation: as evidence that God was actively at work to establish his kingdom, not in some far-off aeon beyond history but precisely within imminent historical time. Newman Smyth, a Congregational pastor in New Haven, Connecticut, was so exhilarated by the new science that he took a leave of absence from his pastorate in order to do research in the laboratories of Yale. In an 1879 book entitled *Old Faiths in New Light*, which was one of the earliest efforts to reconcile Christian theology and the new knowledge, Smyth wrote about what he viewed as the coincidence of scientific investigation with the discovery of spiritual truth:

> The . . . thirst for the real led me away somewhat from the field of theological studies in the endeavor to find what could be known, how near towards ultimates we might come through scientific researches. The early fruits of these inquiries in what has now become the voluminous department of physiological psychology, were then accessible and a better understanding of Darwinism was becoming prevalent in Christian apologetics. These recent investigations and every advance of science towards the origin of things, every ascer-

tained fact far out on the border line between the known and the unknown, had for me a fascinating attraction, as indeed pursuits of spiritual truth in this direction has been to me since—much more than dogmatic theology—my chief study and delight.[1]

Exulting not in scientific discovery but in palpable advances in human fraternity, Ozora Davis could hymn in 1909, and generations of mainstream Protestant church men and women then and later could sing with him,

> At length there dawns the glorious day
>> By prophets long foretold;
> At length the chorus clearer grows
>> That shepherds heard of old.
> The dawning day of brotherhood
>> Breaks on our eager eyes,
> And human hatreds flee before
>> The radiant eastern skies.

A Protestant publication, originally founded in 1884 as *The Christian Oracle,* was renamed in 1900, in prophetic expectation that the twentieth century would be *The Christian Century.* It became the leading journalistic voice of the theological movement that came to be known, variously, as "liberalism" or "modernism," and that, in its earlier years, called itself the "new theology": the effort throughout the major Protestant denominations to reformulate the Christian faith in terms that were consonant with the nineteenth century's achievements in science and technology, in social progress, and in scholarship.

Not that this new theology was merely a kind of sanctified secularism. On the contrary, its religious source was to be found in the fervent Christian revivalism of the Great Awakenings in the eighteenth and early nineteenth centuries; in the evangelical preaching of Dutch Reformed pastor Theodore Frelinghuysen, Congregationalist Jonathan Edwards, Presbyterian Gilbert Tennant, Quaker John Woolman, Methodist George Whitefield, and Baptist Isaac Backus. Later preachers in the evangelical tradition were Presbyterian Charles Finney and Congregationalists Timothy Dwight, Nathanael Taylor, and Lyman Beecher.

In *The Kingdom of God in America*, H. Richard Niebuhr identified the themes that could be heard over and over in the preaching of these earnest revivalists and that were to echo strongly in the new theology. One was God's present rule in human life, and in nature and history as well, thereby conferring a sacramental significance on the whole of creation because it has its source in a common Creator. Another was emphasis on an immediate knowledge and experience of God in the person of Jesus Christ that convinces the mind, regenerates the emotions, and makes possible genuine Christian freedom by "the expulsive power of a new affection." Still other themes were the reign of Christ in the hearts of individual men and women who, in gratitude for God's redeeming love, give themselves to an active charity that is concerned for bodies as for souls, for slaves as for freemen, for aliens as for fellow countrymen; and a coming visible rule of God to be established on the earth.

What impressed the shapers of a new theology was the way in which—providentially, in their view—the secular developments of the nineteenth century were being confirmed by, and in turn were confirming, these religious persuasions: The evangelicals' sense of a sacramental world had its counterpart in the new importance and dignity conferred upon natural process by nineteenth-century science. The evangelical affirmation that "the truth shall make you free" had its counterpart in the nineteenth century's growing insistence on unfettered intellectual inquiry and in movements for political democracy. Evangelical emphasis on a charity directed inclusively to "all sorts and conditions" had its counterpart in secular movements for social amelioration and reform. And evangelical confidence in the future, rooted in a faith that God is directing human history, had its counterpart in a secular optimism that arose intellectually out of the concept of evolution, and practically out of the astonishing progress achieved in science and technology.

At the same time, it would be a mistake to view the new theology merely as an unaltered extension of the old evangelicalism. It was, indeed, a *new* theology, given its distinctive cast by the new science, technology, social conscience, and scholarship. If God is really the Lord of history, the new theologians reasoned, then there can be no independent, secular realm uninfluenced by him. As history's Lord, his hand must be shaping and directing these new developments; and if that is so, then to refuse to hear in them a clear call for the reformulation of the Christian faith would be an act of unbelief. It would be a refusal to let God be God, not unlike that first rebellion in the Garden.

So, joining the received tradition of evangelicalism with the new revelations arising out of nineteenth-century experience, the agenda of Christian modernism included these elements:

- an understanding of God in terms of the divine nearness—immanence—rather than of remoteness, more often as Father than as King; God both reaching out and reachable in the life and ministry of Jesus, as well as in the nearer experiences of the believer's own history; God intimately at work in the natural and social process in which we live and move and have our being, with revelation not "once for all delivered" but continuing

- an antidogmatic temper, an anticreedal bias, believing that Christian theology needs continuing reformation and reformulation in response to God's ongoing revelation

- a new regard for the co-importance of human experience and of biblical witness, on the principle that "Scripture without experience is empty, but experience without Scripture is blind"

- an awareness of the human element in the formation and transmission of the Bible and of a consequent distinction between the spiritual truths that comprise its permanent, revelatory significance and its historically conditioned worldview, which is limited and transitory

- a fresh and centering interest in the human life of Jesus, aided by the new biblical scholarship, and a conviction that his significance as the transformer of our lives is not to be found in a primordial character given to him before time was, as the second person of the Trinity, but rather in a human character achieved by him through single-minded commitment to the will of God

- the Christian life understood as discipleship, as living the affirmation that "Jesus is Lord," whose very humanness makes it possible for men and women to follow him
- fresh attention to the moral teaching of Jesus as the content of what it means to follow him; emphasis not only on the need individuals have for moral transformation but also on the moral formation of social structures into a clearer image of the kingdom of God, and of the essential interrelation of the two; and a consequent social agenda that included conservation, economic justice, human-rights advocacy, and (in some) pacifism
- emphasis on the oneness of all Christians through faith in a common redeemer and on the essential unity of the whole human family through the fatherhood of God; hence, commitment to ecumenism and interreligious dialogue
- an optimism rooted in the awareness that God is actively at work throughout his creation, and that the love of God revealed in the life and ministry of Jesus has world-redeeming power.

THE ANTIMODERNIST RESPONSE

Some American Protestants found the modernist agenda profoundly disturbing, even viewing it as a betrayal of authentic Christianity. One of them expressed that disturbance in these words:

> [Modernism's] attempt at reconciling Christianity with modern science has really relinquished everything distinctive of Christianity. . . . [D]espite the liberal use of traditional phraseology, modern liberalism not only is a different religion . . . but belongs to a totally different class of religions. . . . Christianity is being attacked from within by a movement which is anti-Christian to the core.[2]

What was it to be "authentically" Christian, in the view of these dissenters from modernism? Their roots, too, were in the evangelicalism and revivalism of the eighteenth and early nineteenth centuries, but they drew from it a different set of essentials, or fundamentals, as they began to call them. Although there was no formal decision to define the movement in terms of a particular set of doctrinal affirmations, it was common for antimodernists to claim these five as their own: (1) the inspiration and authority of scripture; (2) the deity of Christ, including his miraculous birth and the other literal miracles recorded in the Gospels; (3) the substitutionary atonement of Christ on the cross for the sins of mankind; (4) the physical resurrection and ascension of Christ; and (5) the literal return of Christ in a second advent.

Other doctrines were unevenly affirmed by the dissenters, some giving them more and some less emphasis—for example, the depravity of human nature, the personal existence of the Devil, the literal existence of heaven and hell, the importance of evangelization—but the five listed above were frequently used as identifying marks of "real" Christians and as the basis for the inclusion or exclusion both of individuals and of congregations from fellowship with "authentic" believers.

Among the five, which could have been affirmed by Christians throughout the history of the faith, the dissenters gave to two—the first, concerning the Bible, and the fifth, having to do with the return of Christ—an interpretation for which there was no precedent in Christian history, as we shall see.

The antimodernists argued that it is not enough to affirm that the biblical writings are inspired of God and are therefore to be received as authoritative for faith and life. The Bible can be authoritative only if we go farther and affirm its "plenary and literal inerrancy." As expressed in an 1881 journal article by its chief intellectual defenders, Princeton professors A.A. Hodge and Benjamin B. Warfield, that rather formidable formula means

> that the Scriptures not only contain, but ARE THE WORD OF GOD, and hence that all their elements and all their affirmations are absolutely errorless, and binding the faith and obedience of men. . . . [Hence] all the affirmations of Scripture of all kinds, whether of spiritual doctrine or duty, or of physical or historical fact, or of psychological or philosophical principle, are without any error, when the *ipsissima verba* [that is, the exact language] of the original autographs [the actual manuscripts originally produced by the biblical writers themselves] are

ascertained and interpreted in their natural and intended sense.[3]

This was a pointed reaction against the modernist theologians who had claimed to find errors of historical and scientific fact in the biblical record, who were trying to understand that record by applying to it the same tools of literary criticism that had been applied successfully to other ancient writings, who were making an effort to distinguish between the Bible's permanent spiritual truths and its transitory categories of thought, and who sought thereby to protect both the transcendent source of its inspiration and the human character of its transmission and translation. Said the dissenters, "You can't have it both ways. Either the whole of the Bible is to be trusted, down to its smallest and most apparently incidental detail, or none of it is to be trusted!"

The other peculiar reinterpretation, having to do with the return of Christ in a second advent, was called *dispensationalism*. Its most influential proponents were Cyrus Ingerson Scofield and a group of seven coeditors who produced *The Scofield Reference Bible*, the most widely used study Bible since its first edition in 1909.* The Scofield Bible presented the "Authorized Version" of 1611, adding marginal notations of variant readings from more recent manuscript discoveries, interpretive articles for major sections (e.g., the Pentateuch, the Gospels), a brief introduction to each book, interpretive and summary headings at the beginning of each chapter within a book and over major subsections within each chapter, and footnoted comment all along the way. One suspects that some uninformed readers assumed that the chapter and subsection headings actually

---

*The last edition supervised by Scofield himself was in 1917 (C.I. Scofield et al., eds., *The Scofield Reference Bible* [New York: Oxford University Press, 1917]) and has been kept in print continually since. A *New Scofield Reference Bible*, edited by E. Schuyler English and others, was published by Oxford University Press in 1967, and the *Oxford NIV Scofield Study Bible*, based on the New International Version, appeared in 1984. Editor English was careful to point out that both newer versions are "adaptations, not revisions," and that they retain "the same doctrines of faith" as in the original edition of 1909.

came from the original biblical manuscripts, thus conferring on the Scofield study aids a misplaced authority.

Scofield and his coeditors taught that God has divided history into a sequence of dispensations: "A dispensation is a period of time during which man is tested with respect of obedience to some *specific* revelation of the will of God. Seven such dispensations are distinguished in Scripture." First came "innocency," in which Adam and Eve in the Garden were subjected to "an absolutely simple test" of obedience to God—a test they failed, resulting in their expulsion. Next came "conscience," in which humankind had "a personal and experimental knowledge of good and evil" arising from Adam and Eve's experience in the Garden, and this too failed, resulting in the flood. "Human government" was the third dispensation, established with Noah and his progeny, who were given responsibility to rule the world for God, but the failure of that rule was revealed in the arrogance of Babel with its consequent scattering of the people across the face of the earth. "Promise" followed—God's covenant with Abraham—but at its end was the Egyptian captivity and the idolatries of the Exodus. The dispensation of "law" began at Sinai and ended in the tragedy of Calvary. We are now in the sixth dispensation, that of "grace," the dispensationalists taught, which began with the resurrection of Christ.

According to the Scofield Bible, each dispensation marks a different method chosen by God for dealing with humankind, "and each ends in judgment—marking utter failure in every dispensation." So the present, the sixth, is destined for the same disastrous end, which will be marked by the faithlessness of the institutional church and a resultant apocalyptic judgment. Then the seventh and final "Dispensation of the Fullness of Time" will be inaugurated, in which God will destroy all of his enemies, past and present, in a consuming fury and will effect the eternal deliverance of all of his saints, both the quick and the dead.

If the doctrine of biblical inerrancy represented a decisive rejection of what the modern era was producing in historical, literary, and theological scholarship, the doctrine of dispensationalism represented a no less decisive—indeed, a resounding—rejection of modernist notions of progress in history and most specifically a rejection of the illusion of human progress within the modern era itself. Dispensationalism contained a clear charge that Protestant modernism is indeed the "apostasy of the professing church," which Scofield predicted would signal the imminent end of the sixth dispensation; and an expectation that the final judgment against that apostasy, and the cataclysmic end of human history, may be expected within proximate historical time.

FUNDAMENTALISM

The antimodernist party within American Protestantism, defined peculiarly by the doctrinal marks of biblical inerrancy and dispensationalism, was not called "fundamentalist" until 1920. In that year, Baptist Curtis Lee Laws, editor of *The Watchman-Examiner*, wrote in reporting on a "Fundamentals Conference":

> We here and now move that a new word be adopted to describe the men among us who insist that the landmarks shall not be removed. "Conservatives" is too closely allied with reactionary forces in all walks of life. "Premillenialists" is too closely allied with a single doctrine and not sufficiently inclusive. "Landmarkers" [a controversial Southern Baptist epithet] has a historical disadvantage and connotes a particular group of radical conservatives. We suggest that those who still cling to the great fundamentals and who mean to do battle royal for the fundamentals shall be called "Fundamentalists." By that name the editor of THE WATCHMAN-EXAMINER is willing to be called. It will be understood therefore when he uses the word it will be in compliment and not in disparagement.[4]

The way was prepared for Laws to claim that term for the movement when, between 1910 and 1915, a series of twelve small volumes of essays called *The Fundamentals: A Testimony to the Truth* began to appear. The series, financed by two wealthy California businessmen, was distributed free in perhaps as many as 3 million copies in an effort to counter the influence of modernism, secular as well as religious. The editorial committee was dominated by dispensationalists, and the largest group of essays addressed the issue of biblical authority and inerrancy. Secular issues critiqued by the authors of *The Fundamentals* included the theory of evolution, modernist philosophy, and "worldly" scholarship.

Fundamentalism raised a legitimate and important question: Is modernism fully faithful to the essential character of biblical Christianity? My own judgment is that, in many respects modernist theology was excessive and wrongheaded. If, for example, it was right in wanting a faith that would be relevant to changing times, it was wrong whenever it assumed that relevance would be found by measuring faith by truth norms supplied by the secular disciplines of science and history. Whatever else it may be, faith is primarily the human response to God's initiative in revealing God's selfhood—his nature, purpose, and will. It is formed in the confession that God has been encountered, and the task of theology is to communicate that encounter in intelligible and faith-ful terms. Theology is not made up by pooling our supposed best insights about ourselves and the life we are called to live, even when that pooling is done with the care of scientific research. Revelation is received, not achieved, because knowledge of God, like knowledge of any other centered personal reality, is a gift. It is given in the self-giving of the Other. The theological enterprise, therefore, has an integrity of its own apart from any other human discipline.

Modernism was right in pointing out that vital, concrete historical experience preceded and informed the written accounts of the Bible, that to value the writing over the experience that formed the writing is to do violence to the living truth of the biblical witness, and that the written word can become vital again only as it is translated into experiential terms. Modernism was wrong whenever it assumed an oversimple identity between the Bible's time and our own, between the nineteenth- or twentieth-century biblical interpreter and the first-century biblical witness. Those were very different eras, and it was a modernist failing not to permit

Bible times their own historical uniqueness. The result was that modern perceptions, foreign and wholly inaccessible to the biblical writers—the evolution of natural and social orders was such a perception—were often read back into the biblical record, when, in fact, they were not there. It was said of the modernist Adolf von Harnack, that in his interpretation of the Bible he was like a man looking into a deep well, who did not recognize that the image at the bottom of the well was a reflection of his own face.

Modernism was right in its devotion to the historical person of Jesus. No earlier theological movement could have given so large a place to that beguiling human figure in the Gospels, because no earlier movement was the beneficiary of a historical science so advanced in the sophistication of its critical tools, the range of its documentary sources, and the depth of its historical knowledge. Modernism did not make the mistake of an earlier **orthodoxy** or a later **neo-orthodoxy,** whose affirmation of the theological Christ to the virtual exclusion of the historical Jesus made it impossible to entertain the full, God-man reality of the **incarnation.** If subsequent scholarship showed that the modernists were sometimes mistaken in historical details and frequently overconfident in what they expected of the historical method, they nevertheless set the Man from Nazareth permanently in our midst. But modernism was wrong whenever, in fascination with the human Jesus, it ignored the transcendent significance orthodoxy saw, making of him merely the model man and, ironically, thereby robbing him of transforming influence. The ideal human person Jesus may have been; yet it is not ideals we lack but power. Calling us to throw off sin and guilt and to lift ourselves into newness by our own moral effort will not create power where none exists, and the ideal only mocks our powerlessness. But if we understand that, in the historical person of Jesus as the Christ, God was actively seeking, forgiving, accepting, restoring, and enfolding men and women such as we, and that his love hounds us to the very hells of our own creation, now even as it did then, perhaps something will begin to change in us toward energy, toward newness, toward meaning.

Modernism was right in welcoming the enormous strides made in the modern era toward a just society: toward racial equality and distributive justice and participatory government, toward the protection of children and care for the aging and food for the hungry. And it was right to understand all of those as gospel imperatives imposed upon Christians by the one who chose as the first public definition of his own mission the words of Isaiah:

> The Spirit of the Lord is upon me, because he has anointed me to preach good news to the poor. He has sent me to proclaim release to the captives and recovering of sight to the blind, to set at liberty those who are oppressed, to proclaim the acceptable year of the Lord.[5]

Modernism was wrong when it took a relatively uncritical view of organized social idealism and of social idealists, when it failed to understand that some of the world's worst things are often done for some of the world's best reasons.

A VENTURESOME THEOLOGY

At the same time that it was appropriate for fundamentalists to ask about the continuity between the newly emerging modernist faith and apostolic Christianity, it was equally appropriate for modernists to ask whether fundamentalism was, in fact, the selfless return to biblical and orthodox doctrine that it claimed to be. My own judgment is that, with respect to two of its distinctive tenets—biblical inerrancy and dispensational premillennialism—fundamentalism was as bold a form of theological adventurism as anything on the modernist agenda. Although it represented itself—and indeed thought of itself—as a return to the faith of the apostles, it was, in its own way, as new as the modernist theological formulations and the secularist social movements it so scathingly denounced. Although we shall examine the fundamentalist approach to the Bible in some detail in chapter 3, and its **millennialist** expectations in chapter 5, it is important for the completeness of this brief historical sketch to offer some preliminary observations on both matters.

Biblical inerrancy was and is both the center and circumference of fundamentalist belief. What was at issue in insisting on inerrancy was clearly stated in 1830 by Alexander Carson in words that still echo in fundamentalist rhetoric today:

> If the Scriptures contained one rule of poetry and oratory, that rule must be a legitimate one, or the Bible is a forgery. And if it tells one historical untruth it must forfeit its pretensions in every thing, seeing its pretensions extend to every thing in the book. The inspired writers may have been ignorant of natural philosophy, as the most ignorant of British peasants, without affecting their inspiration. But, verily, if they have delivered a philosophical dogma, it must either be true or the Scriptures as a whole are false.[6]

Given such a view, that to acknowledge even the least error in the biblical record would destroy the credibility of the entire biblical witness, one can perhaps understand the vigor and occasional virulence with which the inerrancy doctrine was defended. Furthermore, fundamentalists have understood from the beginning that if the doctrine of inerrancy should fall, the movement itself would collapse. And because fundamentalists have burdened themselves with the conviction that their own doctrinal outlook was identical with authentic Christianity without remainder, they expected that Christianity itself would be fatally compromised unless it had recourse to an errorless scripture with which to defend godliness against the erosion of ungodly modern ideas. It is surely clear by now that such an uncritical identification and such a presumptuous expectation were entirely misplaced. The ironic result of fundamentalist efforts, reinvigorated in our own time, to defend biblical inerrancy has not been to strengthen the biblical faith but to make it all the more problematic.

Fundamentalism is not a return to the faith of the biblical

writers because, contrary to fundamentalist pretensions, the Bible does not witness to its own inerrancy (a proposition for which I will provide evidence and argument in the chapter that follows). But even if it did, it would be the most elementary violation of common logic—a lapse known as "circular reasoning"—to insist, as fundamentalists do, that

What the Bible says is true without exception.
One of the things it says is that it is errorless.
The Bible must therefore be errorless because it says it is.

However much that flawed syllogism may read like a caricature, it is not. There is no need to caricature what is already so egregious that its exaggeration cannot be improved upon.

Fundamentalism is not a faithful return to an earlier Christian orthodoxy because, contrary to fundamentalist pretensions, there was no systematic doctrine of biblical authority, in the peculiar terms of inspiration and inerrancy in which nineteenth-century fundamentalism cast it, until the controversy with modernism called it forth. The source of that emergent theology was Princeton Theological Seminary, primarily in the period of 1860–1890, and among its chief framers were Charles Hodge, A.A. Hodge, and Benjamin B. Warfield. Contemporary fundamentalism is still dependent on the Princeton Theology and has scarcely moved outside of the terms it set.

As Ernest R. Sandeen has demonstrated in *The Roots of Fundamentalism*, the doctrine of biblical authority elaborated at Princeton by Charles Hodge said, in effect: We know the Bible is the Word of God because it is inspired; that is, because long ago God acted upon its writers in such a way that every word they wrote bears God's own authority. But the Westminster Confession of 1645, that standard of orthodoxy for the Reformed tradition, in which Princeton Seminary professed to stand and from which the majority of American fundamentalists have come, said something quite different, though that difference was ignored by Hodge and his colleagues. The confession said, in effect: We know the Bible is the Word of God because the Holy Spirit testifies to its divine truth in the moment that we submit ourselves to it. Here are the confession's own words:

> We may be moved and induced by the testimony of the Church to an high and reverent esteem of the holy scripture; and the heavenliness of the matter, the efficacy of the doctrine, the majesty of the style, the consent of all the parts, the scope of the whole (which is to give all glory to God), the full discovery it makes of the only way to man's salvation, the many other incomparable excellencies, and the entire perfection thereof, are arguments whereby it doth abundantly evidence itself to be the Word of God; *yet, notwithstanding, our full persuasion and assurance of the infallible truth, and divine authority thereof, is from the inward work of the Holy Spirit, bearing witness by and with the Word in our hearts* [emphasis added].[7]

So Sandeen concluded from his historical analysis that the *external* criterion of scriptural authority offered by the Princeton theologians, located in the interaction between God and the biblical writers, was a nineteenth-century innovation; whereas what was offered by Reformed orthodoxy, going back behind the Westminster Confession to John Calvin himself, was an *internal* criterion: the present testimony of the Holy Spirit when the Word is read and heard.

Furthermore, the doctrine of biblical inerrancy, vividly expressed in the citation from Alexander Carson above and systematized in the Princeton Theology, was also a nineteenth-century innovation. The authority of scripture asserted in Reformed orthodoxy, designated as "infallible truth" by the Westminster Confession, did not require an errorlessness that extended to all statements of fact of whatever kind, whether theological, scientific, or historical. Calvin himself took a less rigid view of the character of the biblical record, as we shall see in chapter 3, and no wonder! What was "infallibly" authoritative was the message of salvation, which is the main business of scripture, and that message stands quite independently of whether or not, for example, there was in fact such a man as Bildad the Shuhite; whether or not the Jewish hero Daniel actually wrote the book that bears his name; whether or not the original creation was accomplished by God in six twenty-four-hour days. Given the static Princeton doctrine of inspiration, in which authority is invested individually and collectively in the actual words of the Bible, it is understandable that no false word may be admitted, lest the whole structure of scriptural authority collapse. But in the dynamic doctrine espoused by Calvin and set as a standard in the Westminster Confession, the truth of scripture lies in the persuasion of the Holy Spirit. In that doctrine, it is not we who discriminate between what is and is not saving truth in the Bible; it is the Holy Spirit who testifies in and to us. Hence, Calvinist "infallibility" bears no relation to Princetonian "inerrancy."

As the era moved on, the discovery by modernist scholars of historical and textual discrepancies in the Bible becoming more and more intense, and the Princeton formulation seeming less and less effective as a counterforce, one more innovation—this one having the marks of daring and desperation upon it—appeared under the collective aegis of Charles Hodge, A.A. Hodge, and Benjamin B. Warfield. It was this: The inerrancy doctrine can be affirmed only with respect to the original autographs—that is, to the manuscripts as they came immediately from the hands of the biblical writers themselves—and does not extend to the process of biblical preservation, transmission, and translation. On this view, if discrepancies are found in the Bible as we presently have it, they do not compromise the claim that God inspired the biblical writers, who in turn delivered a product free from error, whatever may have been its fortunes since.

Again, as Sandeen has pointed out, this doctrinal innovation stands in direct contradiction to Reformed orthodoxy as codified in the Westminster Confession, which says unequivocally:

The Old Testament in Hebrew . . . and the New Testament in Greek . . . *being immediately inspired by God, and by his singular care and providence kept pure in all ages,* are therefore authentical [emphasis added].[8]

Warfield, for his part, urged that instances of reputedly

discrepant material be taken seriously; but they should be accepted as evidence of scriptural error only

> if the true sense of some part of the original autograph is directly and necessarily inconsistent with some certainly known fact of history, or truth of science, or some other statement of Scripture certainly ascertained and interpreted. We believe that it can be shown that this has never yet been successfully done in the case of one single alleged instance of error in the WORD OF GOD.[9]

Of course not! How could it be successfully shown that there are direct and necessary inconsistencies between present copies, on the one hand, and the original manuscripts, on the other, when the latter disappeared 1,900 years ago? So the Princeton theologians, and their contemporary fundamentalist followers, offer us a doctrine of inerrancy on terms that cannot possibly be refuted but that are of no help at all in responding to the practical problems faced by an ordinary Christian, whether in the nineteenth century or the twentieth, when he or she opens the Bible and begins to read.

Dispensationalism—that framework of biblical interpretation leading to an imminent expectation that Christ will return to earth cataclysmically at the end of this sixth and final period of human history—is the other peculiar doctrinal pivot on which much of fundamentalist belief has turned. The historian George Marsden has said that "dispensationalism . . . gave fundamentalism its characteristic hue." The idea that God has dealt with humankind differently at different times in human history—has set special terms for the divine-human relationship at critical moments, imposing special obligations on both parties—was a common theme in both Old and New Testaments. Similarly, millennialism—the expectation of Christ's return to earth—has also been a persistent theme of Christian belief going back to the New Testament period itself. What was innovative in nineteenth century dispensationalism was the idiosyncratic—and, in terms of biblical evidence, quite problematic—way those two themes were shaped and brought together: a total pessimism about human history, interpreting the past as an unrelieved sequence of moral and spiritual disasters in spite of God's periodic effort to set an achievable standard for humankind; an anticipation that this present dispensation of "grace" is doomed to fail like all of the others, irrespective of any good-faith efforts Christians might make to prevent that failure; an expectation that, in fact, the way to destruction will be led by a faithless denominational Christianity; and a conviction, all of these things taken into account, that there is no hope for the world whatever short of the imminent return of Christ.

Says the historian Martin Marty, "Millennial ideas were as old as Christianity, but this very particular set of them may be traced back to the cottage of Margaret McDonald of Scotland, who just before 1830 claimed visions of the end of time." Dispensationalism's lineage runs from Margaret McDonald and John Nelson Darby, an Irish Anglican turned Plymouth Brethren; American Presbyterian James H. Brookes; and Brookes's protégé, Congregationalist C.I. Scofield, who made it the centerpiece of his Study Bible.

There is no evidence that the writers of the New Testament read sacred history through the kind of dispensational lens that was ground to precision by Scofield and his editors. The term dispensation is found only four times in the King James Version, all occurring in the letters of Paul, and only one of those—Ephesians 1:10—bears any conceivable relation to the scheme that had its modest beginnings in the McDonald cottage. The most distinctively biblical term for the special relationship into which God entered—for example, with Noah, Abram, Moses, and David—was "covenant," a term with which the New Testament writers were familiar and which decisively shaped their historical understandings; but they never built upon the idea of covenant a grand plan projecting an end to history around the year 2000, as Darby and his successors did with the idea of dispensation. Covenant and dispensation are not the same, and the fact that the early Christians interpreted God's relation to history in covenantal terms does not permit the conclusion that they knew anything of a dispensational scheme such as that proclaimed in the Scofield Bible. There appears to be no alternative except to say plainly that, rather than being clearly announced by the writers of scripture, dispensationalism has been forcibly imposed on scripture, and the result is procrustean.

A particularly telling instance of this procrustean willingness to force the Bible to fit the dispensationalists' scheme—one that scandalized many of their evangelical brethren—is found in the place given to the active life and ministry of Jesus within that scheme. For some strange reason, never adequately explained by the dispensationalists themselves, the whole of that life and ministry, including Jesus' reinterpretation of the Law of Moses in the Sermon on the Mount, his teaching about the unlimited love of God, and his call to all to live the life of love in imitation of and gratitude for God's own love—*all of that the dispensationalists located within the dispensation of the Law,* the age of the Old Israel that began with Moses on Mount Sinai. The dispensation of Grace, inaugurating the age of the church, which is sometimes identified as the New Israel, did not begin until the resurrection.

What justification could there possibly be for including Jesus' grace-ful teaching about, and his gracious ministry in behalf of, a grace-bestowing God within the dispensation of the Law? None at all, if one permitted the New Testament itself to make the determination. Without being unfair to the dispensationalists, we may suspect that the contrived logic of their system intruded here, contradicting the plain theological logic of the Gospels themselves. Said C.I. Scofield in explaining what dispensations are: "These periods are marked off in Scripture by some change in God's method of dealing with mankind . . . . *and each ends in judgment— marking utter failure in every dispensation* [emphasis added]." Two formal requirements mark the scheme: When all is done, there must be seven dispensations (the dispensationalists were avid numerologists, and seven signifies completeness), and each must end in a public climax of massive and tragic significance (explusion from Eden, the flood, the scattering of the peoples after the arrogance of Babel, the forty years of faithless and idolatrous wandering climaxed at Sinai).

The fifth dispensation—Law—began in Moses' encounter with God on Mount Sinai; the sixth—the age of Grace—was to be marked from the morning of Jesus' resurrection. If the fifth were to end like all of the others, as Scofield insisted it must, with a climax of massive and tragic significance, the crucifixion was the only acceptable candidate history offered. So it is impossible to escape the conclusion that it was the logic of the dispensationalists' system that shut Jesus out of the age of Grace.

Not that Grace, which is also the age of the church, had much to commend it, in the view of Scofield and his coreligionists. The true church, they were sure, is a spiritual presence bearing no resemblance whatever to organized, institutional Christianity. Dispensationalist teachers charged that the mainline churches were riddled with heresy and predicted that the sixth dispensation would end in a blatant display of apostasy by the leaders of those churches, so much so that it was thought the Anti-Christ might rise from among them. Dispensationalism had the effect of encouraging its followers to separate themselves from the established denominations and to come together in fellowships of "true" belief in order to save themselves from the destruction to come. So, although fundamentalism has occasionally taken denominational form (for example, the Lutheran Missouri Synod and the Southern Baptist Convention in recent years), its characteristic form is the independent fellowship of like-minded believers who pride themselves on their separation from all forms of spiritual contamination, a characteristic that can be traced to early dispensationalist influence. Fundamentalism's apparent eagerness for schism, separating even from other fundamentalists for reasons that often seem inconsequential or obscure to the outsider, has become a standard feature of the fundamentalist phenomenon and figures importantly in the analysis of its political activities and prospects in chapter 3.

Was dispensationalism a nineteenth-century innovation?

Says Martin Marty, reflecting on the odd location of Jesus' ministry in its schema and on its "holier-than-thou" ecclesiastical politics: "No other Christians believed what the minority gathered under this **carapace** did."

Perhaps the most telling evidence of dispensationalism's late origins is its dependence on the doctrine of biblical inerrancy, which has already been identified as a nineteenth-century construct. In fact, dispensationalists were even more rigid in their biblical views than many of their fundamentalist brethren. Not only must the Bible be errorless, in their view, but it must be read literally, without recourse to the poetic or allegorical interpretations that had been utilized in the earliest period of Christian history and since and that were permitted even by some fundamentalist readers. If the millennial anticipations of the Old and New Testaments were to be read in such a way as to permit an accurate identification of the signs of the end times, and a reliable prediction of when the end itself will occur, there must be no ambiguity admitted to the biblical record. There, Israel must always be understood as meaning Israel, never as the church; a day must always be understood as a literal period of twenty-four hours, never as the psalmist's more poetic notion that a thousand years are but a day as God counts time; and a year must always be understood as a period of twelve ordinary months. Without such predictable assurance, prophecy fails.

While not rejecting the idea that, in places, biblical writers may have intended to use figurative language, dispensationalists insisted that "prophecies are to be *normally* interpreted (i.e., according to the received laws of language) . . . that which is manifestly literal being regarded as literal, that which is manifestly figurative being so regarded," as one of them wrote. The possibility that a biblical writer's intent might itself be ambiguous, with interpretation of what is its "manifest" intent lying in the eye of the beholder, seems not to have given dispensationalists a moment's hesitation.

So far were nineteenth-century evangelicals from viewing this literalism as an orthodox method of biblical interpretation, that one of them wrote in *The Princeton Review* in

1853, "Millenarianism has grown out of a new 'school of Scripture interpretation' and its laws of interpretation are so different from the old, that the Bible may almost be said to wear a new visage and speak with a new tongue, a tongue not very intelligible in many of its utterances, to the uninitiated."

DIVISIVE ISSUES: DISPENSATIONALISM AND PENTECOSTALISM

In fact, there was far from unanimous agreement, even within fundamentalism, that one or the other of its defining doctrinal characteristics really represented a recovery of authentic apostolic Christianity. Dispensationalism had its doubters and detractors, not only among nineteenth-century evangelicals, as indicated in the citation immediately above, but among acknowledged fundamentalists themselves. Although premillennialism—the expectation that Christ will return to earth prior to a thousand-year period of peace and prosperity that will begin once God has dispatched his enemies at Armageddon—has been a mark of fundamentalism since its inception, and although dispensationalism has been the most influential form of that expectation, not all fundamentalists have accepted the dispensational scheme. Dwight L. Moody has been described by Ernest Sandeen as the most influential clergyman in the last two decades of the nineteenth century. Moody founded the Northfield Conferences on prophecy and the Bible, one of the chief centers from which the doctrines of biblical inerrancy and premillennialism were disseminated after 1880. He was also instrumental in giving momentum to a movement to establish Bible institutes across the country, partly as a strategy to break the monopoly of established seminaries that were thought to have been captured by modernist influence and partly as places to train lay missionaries and evangelists. Chicago's Moody Bible Institute was named for him and became a preeminent center for the training of fundamentalist lay and clerical leadership. Although the Northfield Conferences, and later the Moody Bible Institute, propagated the dispensationalist view—the institute's dean was one of the Scofield Bible's editors—Moody himself never found that form of the millennial doctrine persuasive enough to embrace.

Perhaps the most intellectually distinguished nondispensationalist among 1920s fundamentalists was J. Gresham Machen, a scholar who left the Princeton Theological Seminary faculty because he considered that it had departed from the strict biblical inerrancy views of Hodge and Warfield. Machen's 1923 book, *Christianity and Liberalism*, was the leading critique of the modernist movement, persuading not only fundamentalists but even so prominent a secular thinker as Walter Lippmann that liberalism was not merely a Christian heresy but an entirely new and antithetical form of religion. While clearly identifying himself as a millenarian, Machen wrote that anyone who accepted the interpretive commentary of the Scofield Bible "is seriously out of accord with the Reformed Faith" and that the dispensationalism the Scofield Bible teaches "seems to us to be quite contrary to the system of doctrine taught in the Westminster Standards" of Machen's Orthodox Presbyterianism. One feature of dispensationalism rejected by Machen was its unrelieved pessimism about the present age:

> A large number of Christian people believe that when evil has reached its climax in the world, the Lord Jesus will return to this earth in bodily presence to bring about a reign of righteousness that will last a thousand years, and that only after that period the end of the world will come. This belief is an error arrived at by a false interpretation of the Word of God; we do not think that the prophecies of the Bible permit so definite a mapping out of future events. The Lord will come again, and it will be no mere "spiritual" coming in the modern sense—so much is clear—but that so little will be accomplished by the present dispensation of the Holy Spirit and so much will be left to be accomplished by the Lord in bodily presence—such a view we cannot find to be justified by the words of Scripture.[10]

If dispensationalism was a serious error, Machen did not consider it a "deadly" error, and he was able to associate

himself with the premillenarians for the sake of other fundamental doctrinal persuasions he and they held in common.

There is another major point of intrafundamentalist disagreement, more bitterly divisive than the dispensationalist
issue. Although all fundamentalists have been agreed on the
doctrine of biblical inerrancy, not all of them have accepted
the view that the Bible is the *sole* source of saving truth—the
principle Martin Luther called *sola scriptura.* In the last
decade of the 1800s, several denominations were formed
that came to be known by the generic term **Pentecostal,**
because they traced their peculiar practices back to the experience of the first apostles on the day of Pentecost, as recorded in the second chapter of Acts. The apostles were in
meeting together after Christ's ascension, when suddenly
there came among them the sound of a "mighty wind" that
filled the house, and "tongues of fire" came to rest on each of
them. "And they were filled with the Holy Spirit and began
to speak in other tongues, as the Spirit gave them utterance."

Although speaking in tongues was apparently common in
New Testament times after Pentecost—Paul's famous chapter
on love, 1 Corinthians 13 ("If I speak in the tongues of men
and of angels . . .") and the chapter that follows give major
attention to the phenomenon—such utterance was rare in
later Christian history. Biblicist fundamentalists—that is,
those who were not of Pentecostal persuasion and practice—
concluded that, having moved the apostles to produce a
written scripture containing all of the truth needed for our
saving health, God had no further need for direct, immediate
communication by means of Spirit possession once the
apostolic period was over. Other nineteenth-century Christians were not so sure. A fresh experience of ecstatic utterance began in 1830 in the same cottage owned by
Margaret McDonald in which dispensationalism was born,
and the spark of that fire was carried from there by John
Nelson Darby and his coreligionists as a companion and a
seal for their millennialism. This renewal of speaking in
tongues, some 1,700 years after the close of the apostolic age,
and the acts of healing, the reported performance of miracles, and the interpretations of signs and prophecies that

accompanied that speaking, were seen by dispensationalists as certain evidence from God that they were, indeed, living in the end times. The practice became more common as the nineteenth century rushed to judgment in World War I, spawning among others the Pentecostal Churches of America, the Church of the Nazarene, and the Fire-Baptized Holiness Church.

In the present era, mutual antagonism between Pentecostals and biblicists marks the most serious division within the fundamentalist movement. While holding to biblical inerrancy, Pentecostals claim that God had no intention of abandoning speaking in tongues at the conclusion of the apostolic period, that he meant it to be a continuing gift to devout believers, and that, by repudiating it, their biblicist detractors miss the fullness of the real apostolic experience and lost vital spiritual power to preach and convert. Biblicists, for their part, believe that, rather than being a return to authentic apostolic experience, speaking in tongues is a direct work of the Devil or a product of modern demonic psychology because its claim to direct communication with the Holy Spirit supplants dependence on the sole, permanent, and sufficient authority of God's word given in scripture and affirmed by scripture itself. The biblicist Jerry Falwell has said that he would never allow a speaker in tongues to preach in his pulpit, and the Dallas Baptist Association voted to exclude churches that allow speakers in tongues in their membership. Fundamentalists like Falwell are also embarrassed by Pentecostal claims to miracle-working power. Pentecostal Pat Robertson says he averted hurricane devastation in Tidewater Virginia by rebuking the storm and sending it back out to sea. Pentecostal Oral Roberts scandalized many fundamentalists with the claim that, when a person died during the course of one of his preaching services, Roberts had to "stop and go back in the crowd and raise the dead person so I could go ahead with the service." Pentecostals Jimmy Swaggart, Kenneth Copeland, and Ernest Angley make faith healing a centerpiece of their televised rallies, to the vast discomfort of biblicists.

So, with no help at all from its liberal critics, each party within fundamentalism anathematizes the other, on the ground that it does not represent an authentic return to primitive Christianity.

THE FUNDAMENTALIST STYLE

The touchstone of the Protestant liberal at the end of the nineteenth century was spiritual progressivism, rooted in a conviction that the divine-human partnership was opening up unlimited possibilities for human beatitude within the present era of world history. This view was given apparent validation by an understanding of history shaped by evolutionary categories.

The touchstone of the nineteenth-century fundamentalist was spiritual **atavism,** rooted in a conviction that world history will reach its final end in human disaster and terrible divine judgment at the end of this present era. This view was given apparent validation by an understanding of history shaped by dispensationalist categories.

Without intending to confer either praise or blame, it can be said that liberalism was thus anticipatory, while fundamentalism was reactionary. The cry of the liberal was, "Onward to the progressively realized kingdom of God within living history!" The cry of the fundamentalist was, "Back to the once-for-all-delivered word of God in preparation for the imminent end of history!"

Each was disablingly wrong. The shallowness of the liberal optimism was mercilessly exposed by the brutalisms of 1914–1918. In 1909 it had seemed unexceptionable for Ozora Davis to sing that "The dawning day of brotherhood/ breaks on our eager eyes,/and human hatreds flee before/the radiant eastern skies." But beginning in 1914, the radiance of the eastern skies was blotted out by the clouds of a war of unprecedented scope and cruelty, and human hatreds, which earlier had seemed to be in flight, were now found to be in aggressive countermarch. After 1918, Protestant liberalism was never again able to recover its original cultural optimism, or to underestimate the collective power of sin and evil in human life.

Liberalism's error was in its reading of the future. Fundamentalism's error was in its reading of the past, as has been shown in the immediately preceding section of this chapter. In its doctrine of biblical inerrancy and its millenarian expectation (and, as will be seen in chapter 4, in its politics), fundamentalism attempted a "return" to the biblical and orthodox past, not as it was but as fundamentalists wished it had been.

Given the evident intelligence of nineteenth-century fundamentalist leaders and their present-day successors, one may well wonder how an argument so patently disjunctive and so offensive to ordinary God-given logic as that of the "original autographs" theory of biblical inerrancy could possibly have arisen and persisted. I suspect that intense emotion—anger, outrage, fear, desperation—clouded then, and continues to cloud, the fundamentalist vision. As the nineteenth century progressed and became the twentieth, fundamentalists grew increasingly agitated at the reformulation of Christian faith proposed by the liberal theologians and more and more alarmed at the historical momentum that was transforming familiar and reliable social mores and institutions into strange new forms and breaking open the comfortable parochialism of the American community to alien influence. In the presence of these threats, fundamentalism sought a source of divine authority for its effort to brake the rapid movement of the times. Its theological strategy was not so much principled as weaponed. It wanted biblical and theological armament for the fatal wounding of its modernist enemies. As fundamentalism mobilized for all-out war, that effort—like every war effort—resulted early in the loss of an ordinary sense of proportion. The tone of fundamentalist propaganda became strident and shrill. Rhetorical overkill became the common mode of attack. Assaults against adversaries were directed not only at what was perceived to be their defective argument but also at what was judged to be their defective moral and spiritual character. Modernist rebels were viewed as the agents of unmitigated evil, the minions of Satan, and the loyalist troops as the agents of unmitigated good, the true soldiers of Christ. The fundamentalist position hardened into nonnegotiability. Its aim was nothing less than unconditional surrender by the enemy or its total destruction. Even Machen, customarily moderate and mannerly in his rhetoric, characterized the struggle with religious and secular modernism in total-war terms, asserting that "there can be no 'peace without victory'; one side or the other man must win."

Other fundamentalists made no pretense at moderation. John Roach Straton, minister of Calvary Baptist Church in New York City and a leading fundamentalist pulpiteer in the 1920s, said this of fellow-Baptist Harry Emerson Fosdick, the leading liberal spokesman of the time:

> We are driven to the conclusion that Dr. Fosdick is not only a Baptist bootlegger, but that he is also a Presbyterian outlaw [Fosdick was preaching in New York City's First Presbyterian Church at the time]; without the slightest personal ill will and with no desire to injure him personally, I nevertheless declare, in the light of Bible teaching, that Dr. Harry Emerson Fosdick is a religious outlaw—he is the Jesse James of the theological world.[11]

And a Baptist publication called the *Western Recorder* observed editorially:

> It will be remembered that the said Fosdick professes to be a Baptist preacher. . . . It goes without saying that Presbyterian cash looks good to him, and withall covers a multitude of Baptist doctrines. Yet, after all, so far as this world is concerned, what is doctrine compared to dollars? . . .
>
> In addition to his other chameleon accomplishments, the floriferous Fosdick is a professor in, probably, the most heretical and heterogeneous seminary in all the round world. There is little doubt that he fills the position without grace but with distinction, to the extinction of the truth of the Scriptures. And while he lacks in the fundamental truths of Christianity, it's "dollars to doughnuts" that he has faith enough in the monthly pay check to deposit it in the bank.
>
> We are told that Esau sold his birthright for a "mess of potage," but this was a mere bagatelle compared to what some men receive for renouncing the once delivered faith. Of course Mr. Fosdick is anxious to please a certain clientele, and surely

he has his reward. It is a safe guess that the spiritually unfumi-
gated Fosdick will not vacate his profitable pulpit until his
congregation "tenders him his resignation."[12]

Fundamentalist rhetorical excess, marked especially by
intemperance and paranoia, became the rule rather than the
exception. It was customary to cast personal aspersions, to
ridicule by exaggeration, and to indulge in scare tactics,
rather than engaging in a careful argument that respected the
humanity of adversaries and dwelt accurately with facts.
Fundamentalists in the 1920s discovered the usefulness of
tarring liberal views in religion and politics with a Bolshe-
vik brush long before Senator Joseph McCarthy made a career of it. Texas fundamentalist Frank Norris wrote in 1923
that "evolution is Bolshevism in the long run. . . . It elimi-
nates the idea of a personal God, and with that goes all
authority in government, all law and order." In a similar but
even more colorful vein, evangelist Billy Sunday said in
1925:

> Our country is filled with a Socialistic, I.W.W., Communistic,
> radical, lawless, Anti-American, anti-church, anti-God, anti-
> marriage gang, and they are laying the eggs of rebellion and
> unrest in labor and capital and home, and we have some of
> them in our universities. . . . If this radical element could
> have their way, my friends, the laws of nature would be
> repealed, or they would reverse them; oil and water would
> mix; the turtle dove would marry the turkey buzzard; the sun
> would rise in the West and set in the East; chickens would
> crow and the roosters would squeal; cats would bark and dogs
> would mew; the least would be the greatest; a part would be
> greater than the whole; yesterday would be after tomorrow if
> that crowd were in control.[13]

In the 1930s, Minnesota fundamentalist William B. Riley
charged that President Franklin Roosevelt was "painting
America Red," adding that "Disarmament," "Interna-
tionalism," and "Social Gospel" had become "passwords of
the secret order which deliberately plots, not alone the
downfall of the American government after the manner of
Russia's collapse, but the overthrow of every civilized government in all the world."

This habit of stridency and rhetorical excess was not limited to earlier decades of fundamentalist experience; it marks the present time as well. The habit is, in fact, endemic to the movement. This behavioral style, accompanied by certain doctrinal persuasions—*indeed, the invidious style indispensably with those persuasions*—is what identifies fundamentalism as a distinct religious, and by extension political, phenomenon. The style is illustrated in the remark by a former president of the Southern Baptist Convention, that God does not hear the prayers of a Jew. Jimmy Swaggart, who has been a leading practitioner of that style, said when endorsing the presidential ambition of Pat Robertson, "For the first time in human history, the possibility exists that the hand that is laid on the Bible [when Robertson takes the presidential oath of office] will be joined to a shoulder, a head, and a heart that are saved by the Lord Jesus Christ and filled with the Holy Spirit." So much for sometime Disciples preacher James A. Garfield; for Methodist William McKinley, whose professed motivation for waging the Spanish-American War was "to educate the Filipinos, and uplift and civilize and Christianize them, and by God's grace do the very best we could by them as our fellow-men for whom Christ died"; for Presbyterian Woodrow Wilson who, when president, once said, "If I were not a Christian, I think I should go mad"; for Baptist evangelical Jimmy Carter. So much, too, for contemporary fundamentalism's favorite president, Ronald Reagan. More seriously still, so much for the view that God saves whom he will, without the permission or endorsement of any human authority, including fundamentalist evangelists.

On a number of occasions during his 1988 political campaign, evangelist Pat Robertson asserted that fundamentalist Christians are more godly and principled, more patriotic, and more concerned about the family than are other Americans. When his partisans out-polled other Republicans in Michigan caucuses, Robertson exulted that it was a victory for the kingdom of God, the clear implication being that other candidates were outside of the kingdom. Robertson told *Time* magazine that, should he be elected President, he would not tolerate atheists in his administration. "I don't think atheists have their act together," he said. Robertson denied to *Time* that he had ever said that only born-again Christians and devout Jews should hold jobs in government, but he was later forced to admit the sentiment when confronted with a transcript of his "700 Club" television program on which it had been expressed.

In the 1986 congressional elections, voters in North Carolina's Fourth Congressional District received a letter from a candidate for reelection that began, "Dear Christian Friend," and that said in part, "Will you help me so our voice will not be silenced and then replaced by someone who is not willing to take a strong stand for the principles outlined in the Word of God?" Its author was an incumbent fundamentalist who had been elected to the House in the 1984 Reagan landslide. His 1986 Democratic opponent, who, he implied, would *not* take "a strong stand for the principles outlined in the Word of God," was a political scientist at Duke University who also happened to be an ordained Southern Baptist minister. When a public storm developed over the letter, the incumbent called his challenger to apologize. "I in no way question your faith," he said—as if ordinary language had no meaning!

Jerry Falwell's excessive rhetoric has frequently made use of military metaphor. "We are fighting a holy war, and this time we are going to win," he has said. In a sermon to his Lynchburg congregation he added, "The war is not between fundamentalists and liberals but between those who love Jesus Christ and those who hate him." He characterized members of that congregation as

> Marines who have been called of God to move in past the shelling, the bombing and the foxholes and, with bayonet in hand, encounter the enemy face-to-face and one-on-one bring them under submission to the Gospel of Christ, move them into the household of God, put up the flag and call it secured. You and I are to occupy until He comes.[14]

In their extremity, fundamentalists frequently engage in the same excesses when anathematizing one another. The evangelist David Sproul described Texas pastor W.A. Criswell as "perhaps second only to Billy Graham in being the biggest Judas-goat of the century"—an odd criticism of one who is as far to the right as Criswell. In criticizing Falwell for having associated with so-called neo-evangelicals who are seeking to moderate some of the more extreme fundamentalist views—not that Falwell was one of them, but that he had not repudiated them—George Dollar wrote that "Jerry Falwell has sinned grievously . . . and continues to sin . . . [and] has become the leading TV Bishop of Compromise, Inc." More extreme is the comment of Bob Jones, Jr., president of the fundamentalist Bob Jones University, who called Falwell "the most dangerous man in America," characterizing Falwell's political maneuvering as "spiritual fornication." More extreme still was a biblicist preacher's characterization of Pentecostal speaking in tongues as "the last vomit of Satan."

This style is as endemic to political fundamentalism as to its religious twin. Robert Welch, founder of the John Birch Society, called President Dwight Eisenhower "a conscious agent of the Communist conspiracy." More recently Howard Phillips of the New Right Conservative Caucus characterized President Reagan as "a useful idiot of Soviet propaganda" because of Reagan's signature on the Soviet-American treaty banning intermediate-range nuclear weapons.

EVANGELICALS AND CONSERVATIVES

All of this is profoundly disturbing to evangelicals and conservatives, partly because they know they are regularly confused with fundamentalists in the popular mind and partly because they reject the adversarial tests of Christian authenticity that are being imposed by fundamentalists these days. Evangelicals and conservatives share with fundamentalists a faith in Christ as redeemer. They decidedly do not share with fundamentalists the conviction that who the redeemed are can be detected by their opposition to the Panama Canal Treaty, to the Equal Rights Amendment, to abortion on demand, and by support for the Nicaraguan *contras*, for the Reagan "Star Wars" defense program, for the unrestrained build-up of America's nuclear arsenal, and for an unyielding approach to the Soviet Union, to name only a few of fundamentalism's litmus issues. Evangelicals and conservatives believe, rather, that these are enormously complex, difficult, ambiguous issues on which no clear biblical imperative can be found and therefore on which those who are equally and honestly devoted to the authority of scripture and to the lordship of Christ will have conscientious differences.

No one has criticized more pointedly—or, one suspects, more sadly—this distinctive pejorative style of fundamentalism than evangelical Edward J. Carnell when he was president of Fuller Theological Seminary. Said Carnell,

> Fundamentalism is a paradoxical position. It sees the heresy in untruth but not in unloveliness. If it has the most truth, it has the least grace, since it distrusts courtesy and diplomacy. Fundamentalism forgets that orthodox truth without orthodox love profits nothing.
>
> . . . Since it is no longer in union with the wisdom of the ages, it has no standard by which to judge its own religious pretense. It dismisses nonfundamentalistic efforts as empty, futile, or apostate. Its tests for Christian fellowship become so severe that divisions in the Church are considered a sign of virtue. And when there are no modernists from which to withdraw, fundamentalists compensate by withdrawing from one another. . . . Status by negation must be maintained or the *raison d'être* of fundamentalism is lost.[15]

One also may suspect that it was reaction against the unloveliness of the fundamentalist style, along with a growing awareness of the moral ambiguity of fundamentalism's adversarial political tests—an awareness that has come out of wider experience with the world unprotected by an earlier fundamentalist separatism—that has led Billy Graham away from his fundamentalist beginnings. In a 1979 interview with *Sojourners* magazine, Graham said,

> There was a time when evangelicals were in the vanguard of some of the great social movements. I think of the fight against the slave trade. . . . Then in some respects we lost sight of our

responsibilities to fight social evils. We said that the world would never be reformed completely anyway until Christ came again, so why bother?

But of course, that was evading the issue. After all, I know that not everyone will believe the Gospel, but that does not mean I should give up preaching it. I know the human race is not going to suddenly lay down their arms, but that does not keep us from doing all we can before it is too late.

Now I think evangelicals are regaining their social concern, seeing that God is concerned about the whole person. There is a danger that we will go to the opposite extreme and reduce the Gospel to social activism, of course. But what we all need to do is return to the Bible afresh—not going to it to prove a point, but seeing what it says as the Holy Spirit opens our eyes. We need to see what it says about our priorities, our lifestyles and our mission in the world.

Then we need to obey.[16]

Billy Graham no longer exploits the cold-war rhetoric about the Communist world that marked his earlier preaching and that is still the stock-in-trade of religious and political fundamentalism. A series of trips to Iron Curtain countries began to make Graham aware of the humanity of America's adversaries and that the casualties in an East-West nuclear confrontation would include those to whom he preached in his Eastern European rallies and whom he was coming to love as Christian brothers and sisters. His sermons, since those trips, include passionate appeals for a reduction in the nuclear arsenal at a time when other evangelists are calling for armed superiority to the Soviet Union. In a 1982 address to the Kennedy School of Government at Harvard, Graham affirmed a personal agenda and adopted a tone not characteristic of fundamentalism:

As a Christian, I believe that God has a special concern for the poor of the world. . . . I believe God has a special concern for things like peace, racism, the responsible use of Earth's resources, economic and social justice, the use of power and the sacredness of human life. I confess that I have not always seen many of these complexities. . . . I am still learning. . . . But I have come to see in deeper ways some of the implications of my faith and the message that I have been proclaiming.[17]

It is this shift toward moderation that provoked Sproul to identify Graham, intemperately, as "the greatest Judas-goat of the century."

In direct reaction against fundamentalism's adversarial and separatist temperament and tactic, a group of evangelical Christians met in 1986 and adopted what they called "A Covenant of Evangelical Inquiry," which is significant for the clear ways in which it called for a different style and tone. It said in part:

We, the undersigned evangelical leaders, renewing our confession of the orthodox truths of historic Christianity and submitting our total thought and action unconditionally to Jesus Christ and the Scriptures . . . covenant together to debate our ongoing differences civilly, honestly and biblically.

In particular, we covenant that as God gives us grace, we will seek to avoid name-calling, and misrepresentation of one another's views. We covenant to practice mutual submission by regularly testing our understanding of the Bible and the world with those evangelical leaders who disagree with us. To avoid name-calling, we covenant together to seek to observe the difference between honest categorizing and malicious stereotyping. To avoid misrepresentating one another's views, we covenant that we will, before publicly criticizing other brothers or sisters, seek to state their views in such a way that accurately reflects their viewpoint. When in doubt, we will directly contact other leaders to make sure we are not misrepresenting them.[18]

In commenting on that covenant, Ronald Sider, a professor of theology at Eastern Baptist Theological Seminary and chair of Evangelicals for Social Action, wrote this:

It is not wrong to think that on nuclear policy, I tend toward a liberal-left stance and Jerry Falwell toward a conservative-right position. But it would be very wrong to ignore Falwell's repeated affirmation of democratic pluralism and the separation of church and state, and to imply that he is a fascist. Similarly, it would be dishonest to ignore my repeated repudiation of Marxism-Leninism and marshal selective quotations to imply that I secretly favor Marxist-Leninist totalitarianism.

. . . we need to covenant to search the Scriptures together. It is a farce to have Jerry Falwell and myself continue forever telling the American public that our contradictory public policy stands are thoroughly biblical. . . . One criterion of the integrity of evangelical political leaders should be a willingness to test the biblical validity of their views with other biblically committed Christians.[19]

In 1921, at the height of the fundamentalist controversy that was then raging throughout the country, Harry Emerson Fosdick, the leading liberal lightning arrester in that controversy, preached a sermon in New York's First Presbyterian Church entitled "Shall the Fundamentalists Win?" A comment made in the sermon states the point of view—the bias, if you prefer—that animates this present work, provides a useful conclusion to this chapter's delineation of fundamentalist beginnings, and offers a transition to the fuller description and critique of contemporary fundamentalism contained in the chapters that follow. Said Fosdick, "just now the Fundamentalists are giving us one of the worst exhibitions of bitter intolerance that the churches of this country have ever seen. As one watches them and listens to them he remembers the remark of General Armstrong of Hampton Institute, 'Cantankerousness is worse than heterodoxy.' "

CHAPTER 3

Fundamentalism and the Bible: The Heart of the Matter

CHRISTIANS ARE A strangely contradictory collection of people. The contradiction is created by the fact that what unites them, makes them a singular and single people, is the very same thing that separates them into contending, often cantankerous, factions.

It is the Bible that both brings Christians together and drives them apart.

The Bible brings them together because without it there would be no witness to the life and ministry of Jesus, no testimony to the Word made flesh, no intimation of that event both intimate and ultimate that is called the Christ. Hence, no Bible, no Christians. Historians of the time, primarily Roman, if they knew about those first-century happenings in an out-of-the-way, wholly unprepossessing outpost of empire, considered them too trivial to mention in contemporary accounts. Were it not for the biblical writers, and for the early Christian churches that preserved and came increasingly to revere their writings, Methodists and Presbyterians and Roman Catholics would not be gathered in congregations on Sunday morning, and Jerry Falwell and Kenneth Copeland would not be on television on Sunday night.

If the Bible thus makes Christians one people, gives them a common identity and sets them out on a common mission, the Bible is also the source of deep, often invidious divisions within the Christian body. Those divisions result in some Christians being called "conservative" or "liberal," sometimes grouped together under the label "mainstream" to designate the preponderance of those who belong to the major denominations, and other Christians being called "fundamentalist," of which Jerry Falwell and Jimmy Swaggart are as good examples as any. Or as bad examples as any, depending on one's point of view, since "fundamentalist," "conservative," and "liberal" are terms of pride for those who admit to them and terms of opprobrium for those who reject them.

THE INERRANCY OF THE BIBLE

What separates fundamentalists from other Christians—from conservatives as well as liberals—is the difference in their views of the Bible. Fundamentalists, as described in the preceding chapter, believe that God is the literal author of the Bible. Those who appear to be its human authors—Moses and Isaiah and Matthew and Paul and the rest—merely wrote as they were directed by the Holy Spirit, so that the sixty-six books that comprise the Old and New Testaments are without error in all of their details: historical and scientific, as well as theological. Fundamentalists believe that *in its entirety* the Bible literally is—not just contains, but *is*—the Word and the words of God.

Edward J. Young has put the case for biblical inerrancy, and what is at issue in fundamentalism's insistence upon it, in unequivocal terms:

> To assume that God could speak a Word that was contrary to fact is to assume that God Himself cannot operate without error. The very nature of God therefore is at stake. If we assert that the autographa of Scripture [the original writings as they came directly from the hands of their human "authors"] contain error, we are saying that God is guilty of having told us something that is not true. It may be a matter which we ourselves could call minor, but in this case a minor error is no less an error than a major one. A person who continues to

make so-called trifling mistakes is not one whom we can trust. And one who constantly slips up on lesser points is one whose words may well be brought into question when greater matters are involved. If God has communicated wrong information even in so-called unimportant matters, He is not a trustworthy God. It is therefore the question of Biblical theism which is at stake. If the autographa of Scripture are not infallible, we can never be sure at what points they are trustworthy and at what they are not. We would then have no sure position for the defense of Christianity. If, as a matter of fact, the revelation of God is not free from error, the message of Christianity must ever remain in doubt.[1]

Fundamentalists believe that the Bible makes this claim of total errorlessness for itself. Paul wrote, in 2 Timothy 3:16–17, that "All scripture is inspired of God and profitable for teaching, for reproof, for correction, and for training in righteousness, that the man of God may be complete, equipped for every good work"; and the author of 2 Peter (1:20–21) insisted that "no prophecy of scripture is a matter of one's own interpretation, because no prophecy ever came by the impulse of man, but men moved by the Holy Spirit spoke from God."

If, then, the Bible makes such a claim for itself, that claim is to be believed, in the fundamentalist view, because the Bible comes from God himself and is his authoritative word. Therefore, not to receive the Bible as a record without blemish would be, for the fundamentalist, to dishonor and defy God, and indeed to declare him to be a liar.

The nonfundamentalist view stands in sharp contrast. It is a strange way to honor God, says the nonfundamentalist Christian, to believe that he would deliberately cloud his word with inconsistency and confusion:

- telling us, in the first chapter of Genesis, that man and woman, formed together on the sixth day, were the last of the living creatures to be called into existence, while telling us, in the second chapter, that man was the first of the living creatures to be formed and woman the last, with all of the others formed in between

- telling us that, after the young Joseph had been thrown into a pit by his brothers because of their intense resentment of their father's favoritism toward the young man, the brothers themselves drew him out and sold him to an Ishmaelite caravan (Genesis 37:23–27), while telling us in the very next verses (28ff.) that, on the contrary, Joseph was left by his brothers in the pit to die and was rescued by a band of Midianite merchants who happened to pass that way

- telling us, in Luke, that Jesus was born at the time of an enrollment ordered by Caesar Augustus, when Quirinius was governor of Syria and Herod ruled the Jews in Jerusalem, whereas the historical evidence tells us that Herod's rule ended in 4 B.C. and that the census in question did not occur until 6 A.D. when Quirinius was indeed Rome's Syrian legate

- telling us, in Matthew, Mark, and Luke, that the incident of Jesus driving the money changers from the Temple occurred at the end of his public ministry, while telling us in John that it occurred at the beginning of that ministry

- telling us, in Matthew 28 and in Mark 16, that when Mary Magdalene and the other Mary came to the sepulchre where the body of Jesus had been laid following the crucifixion, they found the tomb occupied by a single angelic figure, while telling us in Luke 24 that there were, rather, two angels on guard there; and telling us, in Matthew 28 and in Luke 24, that the women ran to share with the disciples the message of the angel(s) that the risen Jesus would meet them in Galilee, while telling us in Mark 16 that, on the contrary, the women "said nothing to anyone, for they were afraid"

- telling us, through Luke's words in Acts 9:26, that after Paul's conversion on the Damascus road, he went to Jerusalem and tried to join the disciples, who would not receive him because of his reputation as a persecutor of Christians, whereupon Barnabas interceded and "brought him to the apostles"; while telling us, through Paul's words in Galatians 1:18–19, that on the contrary, Paul spent fifteen days with Peter on that Jerusalem visit, "but other of the apostles saw I none, save James the Lord's brother."

Such passages as these—and there are a great many others that could be cited—seem less like the inerrant utterances of the God of whose trustworthiness we are assured again and again in the teaching of Jesus, and more like the humanly divergent accounts of the same incidents drawn from separate human sources—sources for which later Old and New Testament editors and compilers had too much respect to attempt an arbitrary reconciliation of their discrepancies; or, in the case of the coordinates offered by Luke to locate the birth of Jesus, like the plight of any author who writes some seventy-five years after the events recorded in his narrative, when the accuracy of historical recollection has dulled.

More troubling still are the moral problems—the ways in which the image Jesus presents of a God who is both just and loving is compromised by fundamentalist insistence on the Bible understood in all of its passages as direct communication from the mind of God. It is a strange way to honor that God, says the nonfundamentalist Christian, to believe that God would

- harden Pharaoh's heart, causing the king to refuse to heed the pleas of the Hebrews for release from Egyptian bondage, and then visit upon Pharaoh and his people the plagues reported in Exodus 7–12 as punishment for the hard-hearted king, as if Pharaoh's recalcitrance were of his own doing

- turn his avenging anger, not only against Achan, a soldier who fought for Joshua at Jericho and violated a divine prohibition by keeping for himself some of that city's sacred objects as war souvenirs, but also cause Achan's sons, daughters, oxen, asses, and sheep to be put to death, though they were innocent of complicity in Achan's sin

- similarly command the total destruction of the Amalekites, who had been troublesome to the Hebrews in their flight from Egypt ("Thus says the Lord of hosts . . . utterly destroy all that they have; do not spare them, but kill both man and woman, infant and suckling, ox and sheep, camel and ass." [1 Samuel 15:2–3])

- command David the king to take a census of the people, in 2 Samuel 24:1, and then, in verse 10 of that same chapter, prepare to punish David for having taken a census of the people

- commend as acceptable the behavior of Jesus, who, hungry and without breakfast and failing to find any fruit on a fig tree, pronounced upon it a withering curse ("'May no fruit ever

come from you again!' And the fig tree withered at once"
[Matthew 21:18]), in spite of the fact, as Mark adds in his
version of the incident, that "it was not the season for figs"
[Mark 11:12–14, 20–21]

- require Paul to say, in spite of Jesus' apparent positive attitude
  toward marriage, that it is better for the unmarried to remain
  so, but that, if their libidinous impulses cannot be contained,
  then "it is better to marry than to burn" [1 Corinthians 7:8–9];
  and in spite of the deference shown to women by Jesus, and
  their substantial and positive role in his life and ministry, to
  say that women should be silent in the church and subordinate themselves to their husbands in matters of religion (1
  Corinthians 14:34–35).

Not only does the fundamentalist view set the Bible
against itself, as the above examples demonstrate—or, perhaps more properly, it sets God's words in one place against
God's words in another place, giving the appearance of a
capricious or arbitrary deity; not only does that view lead to
problems in trying to understand apparent contrasts, if not
contradictions, in God's moral character when the Bible is
taken as a whole, as fundamentalists insist it must be taken;
it also sets the Bible against many of the results of modern
science.

Insisting that it is reliable and infallible in all of its propositions, including those that deal with natural processes and
historical sequences, fundamentalists believe that in Genesis God intends to give us an accurate and adequate description of how and when the earth was created with all of its life
forms, including the human. Thus in contrast to modern
paleontology, which says that the earth is more than 4 bil-
lion years old, fundamentalists insist that it is but a few
thousand years old (the seventeenth-century Irish Bishop
James Ussher said the creation occurred in 4004 B.C.) because
the first eight chapters of Genesis give us accurate gen-
ealogies from Adam to Abraham, and the first chapter of
Matthew completes the tracing of that line from Abraham to
Jesus, all of which yields a calculable historical span. Taking
Genesis as a literal account, fundamentalists identify Eden
as a place that could be located on a map, which means that

the first human life appeared in Mesopotamia, rather than in Africa as the paleontological evidence suggests. Adam and Eve were, in the fundamentalist view, specially and spontaneously created by God to be the sole progenitors from whom all of humankind is descended. Thus fundamentalists deny evolutionary evidence for a gradual development from the subhuman to the human, a theory that would have our first fully human ancestors appearing in several lineages rather than in a single primordial pair. Fundamentalists seem not to be embarrassed by the fact that, if their reading is correct, the human race is the product of an incestuous relationship arranged by God; for, if Adam and Eve are indeed our *sole* parents, then Cain's wife must have been his sister.

Oddly enough, the fundamentalist has an affinity with the view of the secular humanist whom, these days, the fundamentalist loves to hate. Both believe that there is only one way to read the Bible, and that is literally. Of course, the fundamentalist believes that reading it thus literally gives us the reliable word of God, while the secular humanist believes that it gives us a merely human witness of no greater import than that of other human achievements in world literature. I want to insist that both are partly right and partly wrong. If the secular humanist is right in rejecting the claim made by the fundamentalist for biblical inerrancy, he is wrong to assume that the only way to read the Bible devoutly is the way the fundamentalist reads it, and to reject out of hand any claim for ultimate significance made on the Bible's behalf. If the fundamentalist is right in reading the Bible with ultimate concern, he is wrong in assuming that, if biblical inerrancy is rejected, the only alternative is irreligious skepticism.

The following sections will take a closer look at the fundamentalist argument, the better to understand why it is rejected by both conservative and liberal Christians and to discover what alternative views of the Bible will permit us to read it with ultimate seriousness without suspending our God-given critical faculties.

READING THE BIBLE LITERALLY

It is important not to caricature the fundamentalists' view and to understand in what sense they mean the Bible to be read "literally."

When Isaiah writes of the coming time of Israel's restoration, that "the mountains and the hills before you shall break forth into singing, and all the trees of the field shall clap their hands with joy," we are not to understand that passage with slavish literalism, as if God would give the high places real voices and the trees literal hands. When God speaks to Job about that moment in creation "when the morning stars sang together," we are not to read it as if there were a literal cosmic choir. Fundamentalists recognize, no less than the rest of us, the presence in scripture of poetry and imagery that require imaginative interpretation. They know that when Daniel reported night visions filled with fantastic beasts, those visions were to be understood symbolically, requiring translation before they could make any sense. They are aware that parable and allegory are present in the biblical text, and that these too require translation into the terms of ordinary experience. And of course, they recognize passages of description, narration, and instruction that are, indeed, to be read in an ordinary, discursive, common-sense way.

In what sense, then, is the Bible to be understood "literally"? First, God is its literal author. For the fundamentalist, that is not a symbolic or poetic statement but one that means precisely what it says: what the Bible teaches and reveals has its direct and immediate source in God. Further, the Bible is the literal word of God, which means that God is present in it, not as some general principle of inspiration but word by word. We are therefore to read the Bible literally, which is to say, with attention to and reverence for every word precisely because each is a direct communication from God; we are not free to have regard for some of the Bible's words and to disregard others. And the Bible is literally true, in the sense that its entire corpus—whether expressed in poetry, image, symbol, vision, narrative description, or discursive instruction—is to be received and believed because it is guaranteed by the God who is its author.

In spite of the fervor with which fundamentalists affirm God's literal authorship of the Bible, they recognize that there is a problem in relating that claim to any given version of the scriptures. Clearly, for example, there are differences between the King James Version of 1611 and the Revised Standard Version of 1952. Those differences result partly from the progress made in textual study and in the understanding of the biblical languages over a three-hundred-year period and partly from the simple fact that the English language itself, into which the biblical accounts must be translated, has changed. Fundamentalist scholars have themselves participated in some of the technical advances, especially in biblical archaeology and linguistic studies, and those scholars are familiar with the variants in manuscript readings and the difficulties in textual reconstruction that perplex any translator, whether fundamentalist or liberal. Furthermore, fundamentalists understand that translation is a human work, however prayerful and devout it may be. The evangelical scholars who translated The New International Version of 1978 affirmed, early in their preface, that they "were united in their commitment to the authority and infallibility of the Bible as God's Word in written form." Yet they concluded that preface with a confession that, "Like all translations of the Bible, made as they are by imperfect man, this one undoubtedly falls short of its goals" of providing a translation marked by accuracy, clarity, and literary quality [emphasis added].

Given this acknowledgment of imperfection in the process of biblical translation, in what sense can it be said that the Bible is inerrant, infallible? The answer given by fundamentalists is that inerrancy inheres in "the original autographs," that is, in those manuscripts that came directly from the hands of the biblical writers. As theologian E. J. Carnell put it, the original documents were inerrantly inspired in the sense that "none of the biblical writers said anything which was not coherent with everything else written in the Scriptures. In other words, the entire corpus of revelation was preserved free from logical and historical mistakes." All of which, of course, merely presses the problem to a different level rather than solving it, since the "original autographs" do not exist, resulting in the need of translators to depend on copies of copies of copies. How can the fundamentalist argue from the putative inerrancy of the biblical writers' original work to the inerrancy of the biblical versions as we have them today?

First, the fundamentalist asserts that nothing that has occurred in the history of biblical scholarship and translation has successfully challenged any of the basic tenets of fundamentalist faith. The comment made by the translators of the Revised Standard Version of the New Testament is quoted with warm approval, especially since those translators were viewed largely as liberals:

> It will be obvious to the careful reader that still in 1946, as in 1881 and in 1901 [years in which earlier revisions had been made], no doctrine of the Christian faith has been affected by the revision, for the simple reason that, out of the thousands of variant readings in the manuscripts, none has turned up thus far that requires a revision of Christian doctrine.[2]

The present text of the Bible, Carnell and others have argued, represents a self-consistent and valid body of knowledge that assures us that what the Bible teaches is true. One of the things it teaches is its own inerrancy; therefore this affirmation must be true. Since the Bible makes this claim, the only worthy view of God open to us is to accept that claim as true. Either God could have given us such a revelation but did not, in which case he has, by that claim, deceived us; or he wished to do so but could not, in which case he is no longer God. Since neither of those alternatives is acceptable, we must assume that God has both given us a revelation and has guaranteed its truth.

Why, if the original text of the Bible was given inerrantly, did not God preserve those original manuscripts; and why did he not undertake to inspire generations of later copyists inerrantly? For one thing, God's revelation of himself is a work of mercy, not of necessity, and therefore there was no constraint upon God to preserve his work errorless. Moreover, God knew humanity's tendency to idolatry and feared that people would make those autographs objects of veneration. Finally, by permitting humanity to fall into this kind of error in the transmission of the scriptures, God demonstrates how completely sin penetrates human life and how far we fall short of the Son of God.

If God can save us through a text that is not perfect, why the need for an inerrant revelation at all? Carnell answers:

> God could not be perfect and still sanction a revelation which claimed to be originally without error, but was not. But observe that this compulsion holds only for the original writings and not for the present text, for the purpose of the present text is to lead men to repentance, and a document preserved substantially pure is sufficient to accomplish this task.[3]

A NONFUNDAMENTALIST PERSPECTIVE

What is a nonfundamentalist to say of this view of the Bible, which sets fundamentalism apart from the rest of Christendom, orthodox as well as liberal?

The Claim of Inerrancy

First, the Bible cannot properly be said to make a claim of inerrancy for itself. When the author of 2 Timothy* wrote about "all scripture" being "inspired of God," the only scripture that existed for Christians was the Old Testament. Gospels and epistles were accorded scriptural status by different Christian communities at different times toward the end of the first and well into the second century. One of the earliest efforts to compile an authoritative body of Christian literature was made by Marcion of Pontus about 140 A.D. A devoted follower of Paul, who thought that the heart of the

---

*Questions of vocabulary, written style, and the developmental stage of the church reflected in this "epistle" suggest to many scholars that it was not written by Paul himself but by one of his followers, and its authorship therefore cannot be said to be apostolic.

gospel was to be found in the Pauline epistles, Marcion failed to include the two "letters" to Timothy in his canon. It was not until 367 A.D. that Bishop Athanasius first identified the present twenty-seven-book New Testament as comprising the exclusive Christian canon. In any event, the Greek term that in 2 Timothy is translated as "scripture" was commonly used among Greek-speaking Jews to refer to the Old Testament.

The passage in 2 Peter was also written before anything existed that could be called a recognized canon. When it speaks of the "prophecy of scripture," which occurs only as men are "moved by the Holy Spirit of God," the reference is clearly to Old Testament anticipations of the messianic appearance. During the second century, when many churches had come to accept a Christian canon of twenty books, 2 Peter itself was not among them.

If, then, either passage offers any support to the fundamentalist argument, it must be to the Old Testament and not to the New. But in fact, neither passage speaks to the critical issue of scriptural "inerrancy" but only to that of scriptural inspiration and authority, both of which are affirmed by conservative and liberal Christians, who nevertheless reject as unwarranted and unnecessary the fundamentalist notion of a scripture that is free from error in all of its details.

When it comes to a direct consideration of the Old Testament, fundamentalists claim the authority of Jesus himself for their view of its inerrancy. According to the first-century historian Flavius Josephus, the Hebrew scriptures contain the words of God himself; and, said the first-century Jewish philosopher Philo of Alexandria, the writers of Hebrew scripture wrote as they were directed by the Holy Spirit. This was, indeed, the common view of the rabbis during the time of Jesus. It was a view he did not contradict, say the fundamentalists; had he known it to be false, he would have said so plainly.

Arguments from silence are always inconclusive, but in this matter Jesus can hardly be said to have been silent. While it is certain that he held the Jewish scriptures in deep reverence, he was clearly not tied to their inerrancy. He felt free to differ from their precepts when he thought them wrong, and to urge upon his followers a similar nonconformity (healing on the sabbath, gathering food on the sabbath, refraining from ceremonial cleansing before meals, for example). Even more, he declared unequivocally the inadequacy of some Old Testament moral teaching ("You have heard that it was said to the men of old. . . . But I say to you. . . ."). From his teaching we must conclude that he found the Law and the Prophets to be insufficient in themselves, requiring a higher synthesis, which he provided in his own active ministry. The best evidence that Jesus differed from the prevailing scriptural view of his time lies in the fact that his interpretation of that scripture resulted in the charge of blasphemy leveled against him by the religious authorities.

In any event, an argument based on first-century views fails to help the fundamentalist argument measurably with respect to the Old Testament. The Hebrew canon was not yet fixed in the time of Jesus. Josephus was among the first to identify an authoritative collection, which he said consisted of the five books of the Law, thirteen of prophecy, and four of writings, for a total of twenty-two, well short of the thirty-nine for which the fundamentalist view must find justification.

And even if the prophetic "Thus saith the Lord" be accepted as authentic communication from God, that does not by any means guarantee the accuracy of the seemingly endless legalisms of Leviticus or the dreary begetting of Chronicles.

Finally on the matter of biblical self-authentication: even if the Bible did lay claim to its own inerrancy, there would still be a matter of the intellectual integrity of fundamentalist argument at issue here. It is simply not permitted, in trying to prove the truth of a particular proposition, to use that proposition as a part of the proof. Logicians call that "circular reasoning" or "begging the question." Honest argument cannot permit anyone to claim that the Bible is in all respects true and that this claim is proved true because the Bible says it is, since the truth of what the Bible says is precisely the thing to be proved.

The Leap From "Original Autographs"

Second, the leap fundamentalists make, from nonexistent "original autographs" believed to have been wholly without error to later textual materials containing admitted problematic readings from which all extant translations have been made, can be no more than a leap of faith. The argument they offer in support of their contention that the received text on which all translations depend participates in the errorlessness of the original manuscripts—namely, that the present text of the Bible is a self-consistent and valid body of knowledge, assuring us that what the Bible teaches is true, and that one of the things it teaches is its own errorlessness—is simply not credible. Earlier in this chapter, biblical passages were cited in demonstration of the fact that the present text of the Bible is clearly not a "self-consistent witness." Furthermore, as has been seen in the paragraphs immediately above, it is not true to say that the Bible contains a self-consistent witness to its own errorlessness. It may be added to the evidence adduced above that Paul was no fundamentalist as regards his own message. While he says, in Galatians 1:11–12, that the gospel he preached came not from man but "through a revelation of Jesus Christ," and in 1 Thessalonians 2:13, that his message was received in that church "as what it really is, the word of God," it is therefore all the more significant that, four times in 1 Corinthians, *Paul makes it clear that what he is writing in those passages is his own opinion rather than a command of the Lord,* though he believes that opinion to be consistent with what has been specifically revealed to him (7:6, 12, 25, 40).

An Errorless Receiver

Third, if there were to be an infallible revelation at all, it would require an errorless receiver of what was revealed and perhaps even a special language for the revelation. For any revelation to occur, there must be a revealing, an uncovering, of that which was previously hidden in the divine mystery. No revelation can take place until something meaningful has been imparted, and no revelation can have an infallible reception—a meaningful impartation that is not subject to error or even to ambiguity—unless the person or persons who receive the revelation are themselves delivered from any idiosyncratic transcription and transmission of the message that would cloud or alter it in the slightest detail, perhaps by being given a special language that is so precise that it can convey meaning unambiguously.

Fundamentalists acknowledge that, at least in some passages of scripture, God did indeed dictate his own words to the biblical writers, which they then faithfully transcribed. But fundamentalists want to avoid any charge that biblical inspiration was mere mechanical dictation, finding unattractive the idea that God would, in effect, turn men into robots even for the purpose of revelation. So Bob Jones, Jr., while insisting that "God chose the very word that should be put down to convey exactly what He wanted to convey," insisted at the same time that God did not turn the biblical writer into "a typewriter on which His fingers played. God does not intrude on human personality in that way." And John R. Rice, while acknowledging that God dictated the words of scripture, nevertheless insisted that "it was not mechanical dictation." Harold Lindsell and Charles Woodbridge have written that the usual process of inspiration was this:

> The Holy Spirit controlled the authors' thoughts and judgments permitting them to express themselves in terms reflecting their own characteristics. . . . They retained their own styles, personalities and self-command. . . . The Holy Spirit commanded the operation; but Moses, John and Peter remained Moses, John and Peter.[4]

Yet the fundamentalist cannot have it both ways, cannot have infallible impartation to fallible human receptors. Humankind is imperfect and not notably perfectable; even the best among us are given, at times, to carelessness, to error, even to perversity, and view the world with a self-regarding eye even when we are trying to see it objectively. So, in guarding the purity of the biblical witness, it is understandable that fundamentalists would want to find a way to show how scripture could be transmitted errorless through men who were nevertheless in possession of their full humanity. Clearly they have not succeeded. When Lindsell and Woodbridge tell us that the Holy Spirit controlled the thoughts and judgments of the men who wrote the Bible, and at the same time tell us that those men did not cease to be fully themselves, did not lose their personal power or the personality that gave each of them his own style, words are clearly being stretched beyond their ordinary meaning and capacity. If this description were applied, let us say, to a letter of confession that resulted from systematic brainwashing, the clear fallacy would be detected at once. By what stretch of the imagination can we say that a person is still in possession of full personality and personal power when his or her thoughts and judgments are being controlled from some place other than the center of the person's own self, as Lindsell and Woodbridge tell us happened in the moment of inspiration? Such an argument clearly plays fast and loose with words in an attempt to bolster a sagging dogma.

The fact is that if the doctrine of biblical infallibility were to be sustained at all, whether the fundamentalist likes it or not it would have to be on the basis of a mechanical-dictation view, coupled either with an insistence that dictation occurred in a language chosen by God for the purpose or with a Roman Catholic-like insistence that God has given us a succession of inerrant interpreters of the language, ordinary or special, in which the biblical truth has been cast.

We must either assume that our ordinary language is capable of such precise meanings as to serve as an adequate instrument of infallible revelation, or we must assume that the biblical language is a different kind of language precisely suited to such precise meanings. It is difficult to see how it would be possible to prove the first alternative, given the clearly demonstrated frailty of our ordinary language and the sharp differences of interpretation to which the Bible is regularly subjected even by those who share a commitment to its infallibility. And if the second alternative were chosen, it is not clear how fallible humans, inured in their ordinary fallible and ambiguous language, would be able to understand precisely and exactly this special language that would have to differ so radically from the language of every day. So, whether or not the Bible is given to us in ordinary ambiguous and imprecise language or in a special revelatory tongue, it could be imparted infallibly only if there were an infallible interpreter, such as the Pope, who, since the first Vatican Council, has been held to enjoy "through the divine assistance promised to him in Blessed Peter, the infallibility with which the divine Redeemer willed to equip his Church when it defines a doctrine of faith or morals," as the canon of July 18, 1870, declares. Of course, fundamentalists have been vehement in their denunciation of any such special powers claimed for the papacy; and, even though fundamentalist leaders have sometimes seemed to arrogate to themselves a virtual claim to errorless scriptural interpretation, fundamentalist thought has no place for such pretensions.

Thus the claim for inerrant inspiration of the scripture falls of its own dead weight.

An Unorthodox Doctrine

Fourth, the notion of an errorless scripture is not supported in the history of Protestant orthodoxy. If Paul was no fundamentalist, neither was Martin Luther or John Calvin. Luther recognized candidly that there were problems of inconsistency and contradiction in the biblical record. Consider some of the things he wrote about the Bible that are anathema to the fundamentalist:

- The authorship of the first five books of the Old Testament, the so-called Books of Moses, is multiple, and the fact that Moses cannot be cited as their author is of no importance.
- The prophetic writings of the Old Testament were responses to concrete historical circumstances and only later were collected, resulting in some disorder in the text. Later prophets depended on earlier ones, sometimes choosing silver and gold and sometimes wood and straw. And occasionally they erred in secular matters.
- The book of Esther should probably not be in the canon.
- Solomon is probably not the author of Ecclesiastes.

- First and Second Kings are historically more credible than 1 and 2 Chronicles.
- Matthew 27:9 is wrong in its assertion that the betrayal of Judas is the fulfillment of prophecy in Jeremiah.
- The Gospel of John is superior to the other Gospels.
- The Epistle to the Hebrews errs in forbidding second repentance and was assembled from many parts rather than being produced single-mindedly by Paul.
- James is an epistle of straw, having no evangelical character, because it invites us to trust in works rather than in faith.
- The Book of Revelation is neither prophetic nor apostolic and it neither teaches nor recognizes Christ.

As for Calvin, in his commentaries on the Bible he identified places in which he believed the biblical writers to have gone astray. Furthermore, he made a distinction between the Word of God, which is Jesus Christ, and the words of scripture. In themselves, those words are dead; they witness to the eternal Word only as they are vivified by the immediate action of the Holy Spirit, which must do its enlivening work both in the words of scripture and in the consciousness of the believer. Thus it is inappropriate to say, for Calvin, that the Bible *is* the Word of God, as fundamentalists would have it; rather, the Bible *becomes* the Word of God whenever God's own Spirit works its transformative power both on otherwise lifeless words and on otherwise impotent faith.

In some places, Calvin spoke of scripture as a mirror that reflects an image but is not identical with it; or again, as spectacles that permit us to perceive the Word clearly and accurately but are not themselves the Word perceived. In these ways of speaking about scripture, it is clear that Calvin cannot be identified with the scriptural literalism affirmed by present-day fundamentalists.

Nor, indeed, can any other major figure in the history of Christian thought prior to 1800. Contrary to fundamentalist claims, the doctrine of biblical inerrancy as they have formulated it is not a return to primitive Christianity or to Christian orthodoxy. Rather, it was an innovation fashioned scarcely more than a hundred years ago as a weapon to be used against the modernist movement by Christians who were alarmed that the so-called new theology was twisting and transforming the old faith into a cult that bore little resemblance to biblical Christianity. It was, ironically, their own kind of modernism since, as Ernest Sandeen, historian of fundamentalism, has noted, the doctrine of biblical inerrancy with its appeal to nonexistent original autographs "did not exist in either Europe or America prior to its formulation in the last half of the nineteenth century."

AN EVANGELICAL PERSPECTIVE

It is to be expected that Christians of so-called liberal persuasion would dissent vigorously from fundamentalist argument. What might not be expected is that Christian evangelicals would be similarly engaged in dissent on their own terms. Yet a substantial body of evangelical thought, centered especially in Fuller Theological Seminary, has distanced itself from the old fundamentalist categories.

Historical distance is typified in Fuller theologian Jack Rogers. In his *Confessions of a Conservative Evangelical*, Rogers tells how historical research for his doctoral dissertation led him to repudiate an earlier belief that inerrancy was "orthodox" doctrine, standing in "unbroken continuity with the theology of Warfield, the Westminster Confession, Calvin, Augustine, and Paul," and to accept the relative recency, and indeed novelty, of that doctrine in the history of Christian thought—in agreement with the judgment of Sandeen cited above.

Evangelical biblical scholars—Fuller's George Eldon Ladd was one—no longer accept the fundamentalist repudiation of virtually the entire enterprise of modern biblical scholarship on the ground that it demeans the scriptures and reduces them to a merely human achievement; they are fashioning instead a way of understanding the Bible that retains its unique claims to inspiration and authority while, at the same time, they accept many of the fruits of that scholarship. Evangelicals such as Ladd have come to understand "critical" studies—for example, the recovery of the

historical settings of the biblical writings, a greater sophistication in the mastery of the biblical languages, an ability to
test biblical authorship by stylistic and linguistic characteristics, and the ability to identify the multiple sources that
lie behind the first five books of the Old Testament and the
first three Gospels of the New—not as the enemies of evangelical persuasion but as the means by which that persuasion becomes clearer in a text that is vastly complicated by
fragmentary sources, multiple variants of individual passages, and problematic renderings from an ancient idiom
into a modern one.

Evangelical philosophers, such as George Mavrodes, see
the fundamentalist leap from inaccessible autographs, affirmed nevertheless to be inerrant, to the textual sources
accessible to modern translators, also affirmed by the fundamentalist to be errorless, as no leap of faith at all but a
plunge into irrationalism neither required by love for and
loyalty to the scriptures nor dictated by polemical necessity.

Evangelical theologians, such as Daniel Fuller, are now
quite ready to make a distinction between the time-bound
understandings of natural and historical forces that are reflected in the biblical writers—for example, the notion of a
three-story, geocentric universe—on the one hand, and the
timeless message of salvation conveyed by those writers, on
the other. Fuller has insisted that we misinterpret scripture if
we try to harmonize its statements with contemporary accounts of science and history. Scientific and historical statements made by the biblical writers are "non-revelational,"
says Fuller; "they lie outside the boundary of the Biblical
writers' intention, and are therefore irrelevant to the question of Biblical inerrancy." For Fuller, what is revelational in
the Bible—that is, the good news it conveys of God's salvation in Christ—is of unquestioned reliability; what merely
functions to facilitate the transmission of that revelation—
that is, its nonsalvific content—may turn out to be unreliable, with no consequent diminution of the authoritative
revelation thus transmitted.

Evangelical anthropologists, who talk about the problem
of the "indigenization" of the Christian church in non-West-

ern cultures, are now talking, evangelical Donald Dayton has told us, about the New Testament itself as "a particular indigenization and that the gospel message needs to be extracted from first century 'cultural clothing' to be reclothed in that of another age." Specifically, Dayton notes how "evangelical feminists" question "the historically-conditioned character of the scriptures" and worry "that certain ways of reading the Scriptures and certain doctrines about the Scriptures may actually become the means of oppression of modern women by the imposition of first century social patterns."

Evangelical social ethicists—a category that would have been self-contradictory a generation ago—are now saying, also by Dayton's account, "I'm not sure that I believe in a historical Adam and Eve, but I am sure that I believe in a historical application of the Sermon on the Mount." And "Why do our evangelical theologies give so much attention to questions relating to only a few obscure biblical texts while completely ignoring the topic of 'poorology' [compassionate care and justice for the world's poor] to which are devoted hundreds of clear texts?"

As might be expected, fundamentalists have denounced the so-called new evangelicalism as a theological viper in the bosom. Fundamentalist Charles Woodbridge has written that "the new Evangelicalism advocates toleration of error. It is following the downward path of accommodation to error, cooperation with error, contamination by error, and ultimate capitulation to error." In calling on fundamentalists to separate themselves from this subversive movement that has arisen in their midst, Woodbridge declared further that it "is a theological and moral compromise of the deadliest sort. It is an insidious attack upon the Word of God. No more subtle menace has confronted the church of Christ since the Protestant Reformation in the days of Luther and Calvin."

In *The Fundamentalist Phenomenon*, Jerry Falwell attempted a mediating position, reminding his fundamentalist brethren that "genuine Christian people" are to be found in both movements, denouncing what he called "Hyper-Fundamentalism" and "Left-wing Evangelicalism" alike and calling for a reconciliation between what might be termed mainstream fundamentalism and evangelicalism. Evangelicals are not likely to be charmed by Falwell's invitation. Whereas Charles Woodbridge seemed close to hysteria, Falwell was merely patronizing and condescending, urging evangelicals to stop looking down their theological and ecclesiastical noses at their fundamentalist brethren, to stop worrying about academic credibility and social acceptability and what the world thinks of them, and to stop drifting with every new religious fad that comes along.

Falwell's terms for reconciliation are two, one having to do with doctrine and the other with style. "Come back to the fundamentals of the Christian faith and stand firm on that which is essential," Falwell invited (with the clear implication that that is where Falwell himself has been located all along); and the first "fundamental" he identified was that the Bible is "verbally inspired by the Holy Spirit and therefore inerrant and absolutely infallible." Stylistically, Falwell contrasted the fundamentalist emphasis on "confrontation and proclamation" with the method of "infiltration and dialogue" of the new evangelicals. It has been an evangelical error, said Falwell, to "praise the contributions of Barth, Brunner, Pannenberg, and Achtemeier," to propose "a dialogue with Catholics, Jews, and Marxists, among others," and to call for a "moratorium on evangelism in order to study the contextualization of Christianity within existing cultures."

Yet it is precisely dissatisfaction with a rigid biblicism and with a refusal of fundamentalists to recognize that anything Christlike is happening outside of the fundamentalist movement that has drawn evangelicals out of fundamentalism in the first place. Falwell thinks reconciliation is possible because, at bottom, there is little difference between the two parties. However that may once have been true, evangelicals such as Jack Rogers, George Eldon Ladd, George Mavrodes, Daniel Fuller, David Hubbard, Donald Dayton, Douglas Frank, and Ronald Sider, with colleagues Nancy Hardesty, Virginia Mollenkott, Phyllis Trible, and Linda Mercadante, who represent an entirely new breed of women's evangelical scholarship (something which could hardly have arisen within fundamentalism, with its clear anti-feminist bias),* are demonstrating a determination to make their own distinctive contributions to Christian understanding and give their own integrity to a Christian life-style.

READING THE BIBLE WITH DEVOUT DISCRIMINATION

Earlier in this chapter it was said that if fundamentalists are wrong in claiming inerrancy for the Bible, they are right in reading that Bible with ultimate concern; and that if secularists are right in rejecting the fundamentalists' claim, they are wrong in assuming that the only way to read the Bible devoutly is to read it uncritically and to reject out of hand any claim for ultimate significance made on the Bible's behalf. It remains now, in concluding this chapter, to suggest how to affirm that significance while at the same time reading the Bible with devout discrimination.

The error of the fundamentalists, which compounds all their other errors, is to locate the uniqueness of the Bible in claims made for its documentary status. But the central fact about it—the essential, irreducible fact about it—is its witness to the unique event of Jesus, who is called the Christ. The authority of the Bible inheres in that witness and only in that witness. It is to be read with ultimate seriousness only because, in that central and centering event, the men and women of biblical times and their successors through the centuries have known themselves to be addressed by something that lays upon them a claim both intimate and ultimate.

Nor is it only conventional Christians who confess to being touched in that irresistible way. Friedrich Nietzsche,

---

*A fundamentalist Southern Baptist association in Memphis expelled a member church because it called a woman as its pastor. It is unbiblical, said the association, for women to have authority over men, citing biblical support for its view that man was first in creation and woman was first in sin.

who denounced Christianity as "the greatest of all corruptions," nevertheless would not renounce the Christ, acquitting the man of all that he abhorred in the tradition and declaring him to be the only real Christian in history. Frank Harris, who described himself as a pagan and whose debaucheries made the legendary Tom Jones look like an amateur, in his autobiography called Jesus "the greatest spirit in recorded time," confessing that "I have loved him without adoring him." George Bernard Shaw's iconoclasm found no target in the Man from Nazareth; rather, Shaw said that he could see "no way out of the world's misery but the way that would have been found by Christ's will if he had undertaken the work of a modern practical statesman." And the immoralist André Gide reached much the same conclusion, insisting that "if Christianity had really prevailed and if it had really fulfilled the teaching of Christ, there would today be no question of Communism—there would indeed be no social problem at all."

How are we to account for the remarkable impact of Jesus quite outside the circle of faith where we might expect to find it, the claim he has made on lives we would ordinarily think quite impervious to his influence? Perhaps in the same way that we must account for the impact Jesus has had on those who have been drawn fully into that circle. "Unbeliever" and "believer" alike have been drawn to Jesus because they recognized him as the authentic man, the complete man, and because in a real sense they discerned in him the possibility of their own completed humanhood. They were drawn to him because they found in him an integrity that claimed them but which had eluded them; because they found in him a quality of life that, though they had not dared to appropriate, they could not bring themselves to deny. They were drawn to him because he told them the truth about themselves, so that to have rejected him would have been to deny their own essential humanhood. Even when they failed to follow him, they could not fail to acknowledge his authority over them.

The only way properly to enter into the understanding of any work is to respect its own intent and integrity and to approach it on its own terms. The only way properly to approach an understanding of the Bible is to receive it in terms of the central event to which it gives witness and from which its uniqueness derives—the event of Jesus who is called the Christ—and to claim for it no more or less than is claimed for that event itself.

Those who stand historically within the central Christian tradition, both those who think of themselves as conservatives and those who think of themselves as liberals, have understood the event of Jesus as the Christ as the singular place in human history where the divine and the human coexist. In that coming together, the two natures are unconfused; that is, the divine presence in the event does not render the human presence less human, nor does the human presence render the divine presence less divine. The theological term for that coming together is incarnation: God actively and actually present under the conditions of history in the life, ministry, and teaching of Jesus.

One theme unites life, ministry, and teaching: *We are made by Love for love.* Love is the clue to the character of the most ultimate—it is the sovereign power of the universe; and love is the clue to the character of the most intimate—it is the heart of the humanness to which each of us is called. A person unloving and unloved is a person diminished, undistinguished from the meanest object in creation. A person loving and loved is personhood completed, the crown of the creative possibilities God has placed within our reach. What those first disciples affirmed, and what Christians down the ages have affirmed as well, is that in the loving life and ministrations of Jesus we see a loving God himself at work. In some sense we can confess but not explain, Jesus was not merely a paradigm of the divine but was himself the divine lover. As even our own imperfect and incomplete human loves have transformative power, the divine-human love experienced in Jesus as the Christ has the power of radical transformation that, in Christian tradition, has been called salvation. That ancient word means salving, healing; and healing is wholing. Human wholeness is thus the end God intends for us in our creation. So when God loves us in Jesus as the Christ, he gives us the one thing we need for our full humanhood: the love that frees us and empowers us both to love ourselves and to love others, even when that other is the enemy.

To be a Christian is to commit oneself to the love God has given us and the loving destiny for which he has made us. It is because Jesus, called the Christ, is the New Adam, as Paul said—that is, God's new prototype of our own proper humanhood—that he can be acknowledged as Lord even of those who profess to have no religion.

The Bible is not more than the incarnation, as fundamentalists would have it; that is, it is not an exclusively divine work ("The Author of the Bible is the Holy Spirit of God" is the fundamentalist insistence). Rather, the Bible is precisely what the incarnation was: both a human and a divine work, transcendent truth bodied forth in human form. If we diminish either of those terms, we rob it of its incarnational good news; namely, that God cared enough about human life and history to enter it in order to set loose the transforming power of love.

The fundamentalist view is that the Bible, as an exclusively divine work, has necessarily told us, unequivocally once and for all, the real truth about the historical events it records and about the paleontological, physiological, and cosmological observations it offers, and that the biblical faith is thus guaranteed to stand unmarked by the acids of modernity. The secular skeptic, viewing the Bible as an exclusively human work, shares the view that the legitimacy of the biblical faith is tied to its accuracy in historical and scientific matters; and because modern scholarship has shown the Bible to contain historical inaccuracies and to reflect a primitive, naive understanding of natural forces, the legitimacy of its religious assertions is damaged if not destroyed as a consequence.

There is an alternative to those unfruitful options. What the Bible has to say about the *meaning* of our human existence is not tied to having all of its facts straight about the *structure* of our human existence. Science and history deal with structure, what theologian Albert Outler has called *discursive truth*. Faith deals with meaning, what Outler calls *evangelical truth*. On the one hand, structure does not disclose its own meaning, and no amount of objective examination of data in one area of experience will directly yield a comprehensive vision of the whole by means of which to make sense out of all of experience. On the other hand, meaning does not directly disclose structure. No comprehensive vision of life's meaning provides us with definitive information about the concrete structures of life. So each needs the other, and neither can be reduced to or subsumed within the other.

Did the human Jesus believe, in a day before the discovery of microorganisms, that disease comes from possession by demons? Probably, but it doesn't matter. What does matter is Jesus' insistence that God is Lord of the world of disease as he is of the world of health and that God is actively at work in every healing process. Did the human Jesus believe, in a day before the use of radio telescopes, in a simple three-story universe—the vault of the heavens curved just above the plane of earth, so near that the people of Babel could be thought to build a tower high enough to assault heaven's precincts, with a shadowy, dark, forbidding afterworld somewhere just beneath men's feet? Probably, but it doesn't matter. What does matter is Jesus' insistence that the whole of creation is grounded in God, that God is in and under every creative process, and that nothing—neither height nor depth, neither present reality nor future possibility—can separate us from God's sovereign, loving presence.

Science and history disclose the structures of our lives; faith discloses the meaning of our lives. And the central meaning of the New Testament, embodied in the life, ministry, and teaching of Jesus, is that we are made by Love for love. About that, historical and scientific scholarship are dumb: silent and unknowing.

Luther recognized that there are problems of occasional inconsistency and even contradiction in the biblical record, but for Luther those problems didn't matter. The scripture, he said, is the swaddling clothes within which Christ is laid; and we err if we give as much importance to the clothes as we do to the Christ. Individual passages, and indeed entire books of the Old and New Testaments, were to be judged for their importance and ability to edify, said Luther, by the faithfulness with which they present Christ to us.

That is the principle of biblical discrimination I am urging here, in contrast to the fundamentalist view: Everything in the Bible is to be judged for its importance to faith by whether or not it clarifies the central witness to Jesus as the Christ. Everything in the Bible is to be judged for its truthfulness—not its discursive truth but its evangelical truth—by whether or not it conforms to that witness. What fails to clarify is unimportant; what fails to conform is untrue.

The English historian Herbert Butterfield has put this single criterion with simple, unequivocal eloquence: "Hold to Christ," said Butterfield, "and for the rest be totally uncommitted."

THE POETRY OF JESUS' BIRTH

If the only way properly to approach the Bible (or indeed any other work) is to respect its own intent and integrity and to approach it on its own terms (rather than importing alien criteria, as fundamentalists do when they impose upon the Bible the claim of infallibility), the result will be to call into question some doctrines that are dear to the fundamentalist heart, while adding support to others.

One fundamentalist doctrine that cannot stand the test of original biblical intent is that of the virgin birth of Jesus. The problem with the virgin birth, which fundamentalists insist is an essential test of authentic Christian faith, is not that the religions of the ancient world were filled with accounts of miraculously birthed saviors, or that modern science has no place for human parthenogenesis, both of which are true. The problem is not external to the New Testament but internal to it: the New Testament itself fails to affirm the virgin birth broadly or to give it a central place in its witness to Jesus as the Christ. Consider the following points.

First, the miraculous birth of Jesus is reported unambiguously in only one place in the New Testament. In Matthew, Mary was found to be with child by the Holy Spirit, a condition Matthew associated with the prophecy of Isaiah, that "a virgin shall conceive and bear a son." Matthew used the Septuagint version of Isaiah, a Greek translation of the Old Testament prepared for non-Hebrew-speaking Jews. The Greek word for "virgin" in the Septuagint does imply sexual innocence; but the original Hebrew word, which the Septuagint mistranslated, meant only "a young woman of marriageable age." Matthew was apparently mistaken in thinking that Isaiah was looking for a messiah who would come by miraculous generation.

Second, Luke's birth account is ambiguous. While Mary is told by an angel that the Holy Spirit "will come upon" her, that the power of God will "overshadow" her, there is no explicit elimination of Joseph from the impregnation nor any mention of embarrassment on his part that his betrothed had become pregnant without his help, which is the seal Matthew sets on the miracle. Neither Matthew nor Luke makes any later reference to the birth, and Mark and John contain no birth accounts at all. Nowhere else in the whole of the New Testament is there even a hint of the miracle reported by Matthew. If Paul knew of it, he obviously thought it unimportant, for it nowhere appears in the essential apostolic teaching he was concerned to transmit to new Christians in his gentile mission—a strange omission if the Third Gospel is interpreted as affirming a birth miracle, given Paul's close association with Luke.

Third, those with whom Jesus was associated early in his life seem not to have been led to expect anything unusual of Jesus. Nazareth neighbors apparently thought of him as ordinary, so that when he returned to his home synagogue to speak at the beginning of his public ministry, "they wondered at the gracious words which proceeded out of his mouth; and they said, Is this not Joseph's son?" In fact, the Gospels suggest that, in his teaching and healing, Jesus was an embarrassment to his family. Mark 3:21 says that they thought "he was beside himself," that is, mentally unbalanced. Matthew 12:46–50, with parallels in Mark and Luke; Matthew 10:34–36, with a parallel in Luke; and John 1:11, all contain strong echoes of an estrangement between Jesus and his mother and brothers, apparently because they had no preparation, from their earlier life together, for his remarkable, controversy-arousing behavior.*

Fourth, the virgin birth was not a part of the common public message taught by the early post-New Testament church. From the beginning, Christian orthodoxy insisted that if either the divine or the human character of Jesus is weakened, what God has done for us is trivialized. Only if God really revealed himself in real man can there be any hope for the redemption of our human kind: that is what orthodox faith has insisted against those early heresies, and later ones as well, that would have made Jesus less than human. But how is it possible to affirm the full humanhood of one of whom it is claimed that he was born as no other man has ever come forth?

So the virgin birth, as a physiological fact, fails—not out of scientific consideration, but out of the weight of biblical evidence, and by the test of Christian orthodoxy. Rather than illuminating the incarnational good news, it obscures it and renders it problematic.

The stories of Jesus' birth are not lost to us because they lack literal credibility, any more than the parable of the Prodigal Son is of no use to us because Jesus made it up. The birth stories gain a power as poetry they could never have commanded as biological description.

Those who wrote the Old and New Testaments were regularly driven to poetry for the expression of their most profound confessions and affirmations, simply because the literal, prosaic language of ordinary discourse could not

---

*What, we may appropriately wonder, would Jesus himself have said of an account of his miraculous birth, had he known of it? I suggest that, at the very least, he would have kept it to himself. Matthew, Mark, and Luke all make it clear that, while Jesus performed acts of healing out of compassion for human suffering, he did so reluctantly, lest the sensation-seeking crowds miss that spiritual wholeness that was the greater miracle. Word of his own miraculous birth would surely have drawn those crowds to see the human oddity rather than to hear the saving message.

contain the truths they had to share. Literal language is adequate for describing the external, casual, routine, structural conditions of our existence; but the inner world of our meanings demands a richer rhetoric. If ordinary, literal language is inadequate in expressing the depths of human love and despair, how much more frail and earth-bound is it in expressing meanings that reach beyond time to the eternal. No wonder the most moving passages in the Bible are those that rise to poetry.

It is remarkable how much is missing in the New Testament portrait of the man from Nazareth that we would like to know about him. We have seen that most of its writers were indifferent to the circumstances of his birth, and the one who tried to date it—Luke—gave such a garbled account of the historical coordinates that we must still speculate about the year and time. Search as we may through the New Testament, we will find not the least clue to the physical appearance of Jesus. How are we to explain what appears to us modern women and men as a strange carelessness, the omission of so much in their portrait of Jesus that a modern biographer would consider essential?

The answer is not difficult to find. The writers of the New Testament, and Christians of the early church, viewing history from what George Buttrick has called "the favorable side of Good Friday and Easter," believed that they had come into the presence of such an event that their ideas of what was important were radically changed. Not, How and when was Jesus born? but, What new reality was born in him? Not, How did he appear? but, What did his appearance among us signify? That was what they asked; and in the presence of that asking, so fateful for human existence, all other questions paled into insignificance.

And the answer faith supplied was the most audacious affirmation to be found in all of human history, couched not in the frail, literal language of ordinary discourse but in that poetry that was the strongest, the most exalted, the truest language they could find: "And the Word was made flesh and dwelt among us; and we beheld his glory, glory as of an only begotten son from the father, full of grace and truth."

This was no ordinary man whom one asks to fill out a biographical questionnaire. This was the one of whom even the doubting Thomas declared: "My Lord and my God!"

THE CENTRALITY OF THE RESURRECTION

The doctrine of the resurrection of Jesus, held not only by fundamentalists but by the Christian mainstream to be a— perhaps even *the*—central tenet of Christian faith, is quite a different matter from the virgin birth when tested in the light of the original biblical intent. Consider the following points:

First, the resurrection of Jesus was the most common affirmation of the early church. It is explicitly affirmed in almost every book of the New Testament and, considering the church's common witness, can be presumed to lie under those brief, later epistles in which it is not explicitly mentioned. The earliest written account is in 1 Corinthians 15:3–8, usually dated just after 50 A.D., where Paul preserves and transmits a tradition in which he himself has been instructed by the apostles following his conversion. He appeals for public corroboration to the authority of eyewitnesses, who are still alive.

Second, resurrection accounts in the four Gospels differ in their details, adding to the credibility of the central event itself. They display discrepancies one might expect in any happening recounted at a later time from the point of view of different witnesses to it, who remember different things or remember them differently while agreeing on the central event. Discrepancies in these accounts show persuasively that there was no grand conspiracy among the apostles to create a strategic myth as a means of countering the apparent failure of their movement in Jesus' death on the cross, as has sometimes been charged.

Third, in spite of the enormous nuisance created by the apostles' preaching of the resurrection, the Jewish authorities did not refute them by producing Jesus' body.

Fourth, the changes that occurred in the apostles themselves, following their reported resurrection experiences, surely required some radically transforming event as their source. No mere gradual strengthening of conviction that Jesus was right after all can account for those changes. No mere inner mystical or psychological awareness would be sufficient to create in them that unity of persuasion that the disciples exhibited after the resurrection: their radically new understanding of Jesus' ministry and mission, which earlier they had cordially misunderstood in spite of Jesus' explicit attempts to correct them. Even more impressive is the alteration in their characters, after the resurrection, in which formerly weak and irresolute men were now prepared to endure persecution, imprisonment, and martyrdom for the sake of the message they believed had been vouchsafed to them by God's raising of Jesus from the dead.

Finally, Paul placed the resurrection at the very center of Christian affirmation as its sine qua non: without the resurrection, he wrote in 1 Corinthians 15:17, "your faith is futile and you are still in your sins"; and again in Romans 10:9 he wrote, "if you confess with your lips that Jesus is Lord and believe in your heart that God raised him from the dead, you will be saved." The power of salvation, Paul says, is not in the cross, as fundamentalist evangelists have claimed, but in the resurrection.

So, though we may not be able to explain the resurrection event, the New Testament will not let us explain it away. It was substantially real to those first witnesses, so much so that they were willing to die for it. For them, the resurrection was the ultimate illumination of the incarnational good news: as God raised Jesus from the dead, so is he prepared to raise us to new life—to awaken in our dead spirits a new love, one so powerful that death itself cannot defeat it.

CHAPTER 4

Fundamentalism and the Present Age: The Politics of Divisiveness

ALTHOUGH ONE WOULD scarcely know it from the sophistication with which they have learned to organize, fundamentalists are "Johnnies-come-lately" to the field of direct political action.

Fundamentalist Political Conversions

Jerry Falwell, who was the leading national spokesman for the political agenda of the religious right until his announced "retirement" from politics in 1987,* took a very different view of the proper relationship between the church and the world in a 1965 sermon on "Ministers and Marchers." "Preach the Word" is God's commission to the church, Falwell said then.

> We have a message of redeeming grace through a crucified and risen Lord. This message is designed to go right to the heart of man and there meet his deep spiritual need. Nowhere are we commissioned to reform the externals. We are not told to wage wars against bootleggers, liquor stores, gamblers, or any other

---

*That "retirement" has not kept Falwell from continuing to engage in public political controversy and provocation.

existing evil as such. Our ministry is not reformation but transformation. The gospel does not clean up the outside but rather regenerates the inside. . . .

We are cognizant that our only purpose on this earth is to know Christ and to make Him known. Believing the Bible as I do, I would find it impossible to stop preaching the pure saving gospel of Jesus Christ, and begin doing anything else— including fighting Communism, or participating in civil-rights reforms.[1]

Fourteen years later, Falwell founded the Moral Majority, after having organized a series of "I Love America" conferences around the country. In 1980 he repudiated the 1965 sermon, calling it "false prophecy."

One may wonder whether Pat Robertson fell under the mischievous influence of the same false spirit, and at nearly the same time. In the fall of 1966, his father, U.S. Senator A. Willis Robertson of Virginia, sought Pat's help in a difficult reelection contest, but "the Lord steadfastly refused to let me," Pat explained, adding that God told him, "You cannot tie my eternal purposes to the success of any political candidate." When the senator lost the election, Pat did not share his father's deep despair but instead praised God that he had been able to avoid entering the political realm, saying, "Thank you, Lord, for closing this door also."

In 1987, having officially declared himself to be a candidate for the Republican presidential nomination, Robertson, like Falwell, made a 180-degree shift from his earlier repudiation of political involvement, declaring, "I have a direct call and leading from God" to enter the presidential race. Quite unlike Falwell, however, when Robertson was challenged with his contrary declaration of 1966, instead of characterizing that earlier utterance as "false prophecy," he boldly declared that in the meantime God had changed his mind about politics.

One suspects that that tells us more about the difference between Falwell and Robertson as men than it does about any change in the divine disposition.

The attitude toward politics taken by Falwell and Robertson in the 1960s was one that had been deeply engrained in the fundamentalist movement. Earlier in this century, it was a characteristic mark of fundamentalism to demand the complete separation of the church from public life with its "worldly" entanglements. The church was to be disentangled from the utterly mistaken notion that human beatitude could be achieved by altering the external, material conditions of society by political means, while ignoring the deeper need for an inner regenerative change in the lives of individual men and women. It was to stand apart from the taint of political issues that were thought to be unspiritual, if not actually antispiritual, and from the acceptance of, and indeed the demand for, a political compromise that was wholly alien to the fundamentalist style. Fundamentalist preachers and evangelists frequently inveighed against the sins of Bolshevism, especially because they believed that its abolition of private property was a violation of God's law established in the Old Testament, and even against programs of tax-supported public welfare, because they considered those taxes to be a Bolshevist-like form of theft from those who were taxed. But for the most part, their moral critique was limited to preaching against such personal sins as drinking, gambling, dancing, and fornication, which were thought to despoil the inner person, and against such "worldly" activities as the music hall and the motion picture theater, where those behaviors were often beguilingly portrayed. Believing that the world was so unremittingly enmeshed in evil and history so irredeemable that the end of the age was imminent, they preached separation from the world and the need for a spiritual regeneration in the lives of individuals that would empower them to repudiate those personal sins in preparation for the judgment to come.

By the time World War II was over, however, the repudiation of a social ethic and of an attendant social agenda had begun to change, at least among some on the religious right. That change was both signaled and substantially influenced by Carl F.H. Henry's 1947 book, *The Uneasy Conscience of Modern Fundamentalism*. In his introduction to the Henry book, Harold J. Ockenga, long-time fundamentalist spokesman, put the issue squarely up to the movement: "If the Bible-believing Christian is on the wrong side of social problems such as war, race, class, labor, liquor, imperialism, etc., it is time to get over the fence to the right side. The church needs a progressive fundamentalism with a social message."

Carl Henry, who has been the leading systematic theologian of the religious right and later was to become the editor of its most influential journal, *Christianity Today,* wrote that, however shocking it may be to realize that "Christian supernaturalism" [that is, fundamentalism] is now being charged with losing its devotion to human well-being, the truth is that the charge is justified. To be sure, he said, fundamentalism has been militantly opposed to sin, but it has been individual sin rather than social evil. Fundamentalism has been so preoccupied with its opposition to modernism that it has tended to reject the social reforms that were identified with that modernism. Furthermore, millennialism has dissipated fundamentalist social energies. Because the present social order has been thought to have no hope of regeneration apart from the return of Christ, there has been no motivation for fundamentalism to address social evils. But, Henry argued, Jesus taught *both* that his kingdom *is not* here, and that it *is* here. Therefore, "We must confront the world *now* with an ethics to make it tremble, and with a dynamic to give it hope."

Henry proposed a fundamentalist social ethic that is "(1) predicated upon an all-inclusive redemptive context for its assault on global ills; (2) involves total opposition to all moral evils, whether societal or personal; (3) offers not only a higher ethical standard than any other system of thought, but provides also in Christ a dynamic to lift humanity to its highest level of moral achievement."

Henry also expressed opposition to the traditional separatism that has kept fundamentalists from making common cause with nonfundamentalists. Rather, he said, fundamentalists should participate actively in reform movements that are worthy and should "condemn all social evils, no less vigorously than any other group." When fundamentalists are in the minority in such movements, they should retain their spiritual integrity by expressing "their opposition to evils in a 'formula of protest,' concurring heartily in the assault on social wrongs, but insisting upon the regenerative context as alone able to secure a permanent rectification of such wrongs."

Those who adopted the view propounded by Henry in 1947 also adopted more moderate views on other matters, including a shift from the doctrine of biblical inerrancy to that of biblical infallibility, as has already been seen in chapter 2. The moderates came increasingly to drop the fundamentalist designation and to identify themselves by the older and more historically distinguished term, evangelical. Sometimes they were called "new" evangelicals, and not always for the purpose of conveying a compliment. One of the important developments within this new party, given prophetic voice by Ockenga and Henry, has been the formation in 1973 of Evangelicals for Social Action, whose manifesto on fairness in debate on doctrinal and ethical issues was cited at the end of chapter 2.

It would appear that neither Falwell nor Robertson was paying attention while this was going on, or that their consciences were not "uneasy" on the social issues that had come to agitate coreligionists Ockenga and Henry. Twenty years after *The Uneasy Conscience of Modern Fundamentalism* appeared and the evangelical shift toward a social ethic was well under way, Falwell and Robertson were still preaching a politics-be-damned, separatist line. What, finally in the late 1970s, drew them from preaching separatism into outright political advocacy and activism? In *Cities on a Hill*, Frances FitzGerald makes a persuasive case that the change was not at all one of principle but merely of tactic. The shift was not from separatism to involvement, she argues. They had been deeply involved in the culture all along. When, in the mid-1800s, white denominations in the South rejected "politics," that was because "their congregations were more or less content with things as they were." Thus the refusal of Southern white Protestants to address the "political" issues of slavery, and their preference instead for such "personal" issues as drinking, gambling, dancing, and the like, was not separatism, as they claimed, but its opposite. They were so fully acculturated to the mores and institutions of the South that they resisted any change in them. White Southern fundamentalism was, in the fullest sense, a "culture religion"—ironically, the very charge fundamentalists were later to hurl deprecatingly at Protestant liberalism with its affinity for the modern mood.

Southern churches continued to reject "politics" after the Civil War as a means of separating themselves from the slavery of the past and the racial injustices of the present. FitzGerald writes:

> As a matter of theology, Falwell belongs to this southern tradition of pietistic withdrawal. But as a matter of circumstance he and his people belong to the New South and its economic success story. Even in the early years, he never interpreted the doctrine of separation to mean withdrawal from commerce and industry. His sermons were often lessons in worldly success. . . . Instead of urging retreat from the social order, he urged participation in it. His failure to criticize the social status quo—except on the "moral issues" of alcohol and others—thus had to be interpreted as support for it.[2]

Increasingly, however, Falwell—and Robertson, for whom, as a Virginian, the FitzGerald proposal makes equal sense—found in the American culture at large much that alarmed them: abortion advocacy, the changing roles of women, "permissive" sex, secular influences in the schools, a less macho American foreign policy during the Carter years. Civil-rights activism showed, says FitzGerald, that preachers could be politically effective. The entry of Falwell and his fellow evangelists—the more prominent among them are all Southern in origin—into the political arena beginning in the late 1970s was thus not a shift from cultural separatism to cultural involvement, as it appeared, but merely a shift from endorsing the prevailing Southern culture to attacking the prevailing national culture. And the purpose of that attack has not been merely to turn America away from liberal heresy and to return it to the true faith—not merely doctrinal repristinization, as one might suppose from some of the preaching—but to turn America from its evolving personal and social values back to the values, real or merely imagined, of an earlier sectional (i.e., Southern) culture, now torn from its historical roots and presented as God's biblically authorized plan for America.

THE REAGAN INFLUENCE

In the early 1970s, Falwell and Robertson could not have anticipated the rise of a chauvinistic political movement in search of a broadened base for national office, the opportunity that would offer a fundamentalism hungry for the power that had long eluded it, and the way an alliance between the two would change the nature of American politics and their own political indisposition along with it. Neither did others anticipate such an alliance. In a 1972 book on the future of the American religious experience, Frederick Sontag and John Roth wrote: "Our religious situation has now changed permanently, and religion will never again be so clearly identified with national aims as it once was." Yet a mere eight years later, Ronald Reagan appeared before the Republican convention that nominated him and talked about God's providential plan for the nation, inviting fellow Republicans to initiate their campaign with a moment of silent prayer. Once in office, Reagan formally presented the nation with a religious agenda that included prayer in the schools, an end to abortion rights, and a crusade against the Soviet "evil empire." Later, in an address to the National Association of Evangelicals, Reagan said the following:

> The Declaration of Independence mentions the Supreme Being no less than four times; "In God We Trust" is engraved on our coinage; the Supreme Court opens its proceedings with a religious invocation; and members of Congress open their sessions with a prayer.
> I just happen to believe that school children in the United States are entitled to the same privileges as Supreme Court justices and Congressmen. . . .
> Let our children pray. . . . The First Amendment never in-

tended to require government to discriminate against religious speech.[3]

At a 1984 prayer breakfast in Dallas, the President declared that those with a religious agenda are faithful to the nation's traditions, while those with a secular agenda are a source of intolerance in the American society.

So much for the "permanent change" predicted by Sontag and Roth!

The Reagan phenomenon was, in important respects, a religious phenomenon, centered in his ability to forge a persuasive rhetoric of national purpose couched in terms of "traditional" values; in his deliberate confusing of political ideology with sectarian religion; and in his open, even eager, alliance with Protestant fundamentalism and his willingness to risk—indeed, to abet—bitter polarization within the American community as consequence.

Of course, Americans had seen religious influence near the center of national power before, but the Reagan phenomenon was something new. Richard Nixon and Billy Graham were the nation's "odd couple" in the early 1970s, and Jimmy Carter was an evangelical Christian president of evident piety. Yet neither Nixon nor Carter made an overt bid to enlist in his political following an entire movement noted for its invidious animus.

What the Reagan years gave Americans was something odder than the "odd couple" of the 1970s, with Nixon's disinclination to venture out to an established congregation, preferring instead to have Sunday services conducted by Graham and other visiting clergy in the White House itself. It was something stranger than the image of the President being driven regularly on Sunday mornings from the White House to the First Baptist Church, there to teach an adult Sunday School class, which was a feature of the Carter years. What Americans had in Ronald Reagan was a president, rhetorically pious but of no evident piety, and with no adult history of regular connection with any worshiping body, who was ordained to eldership in the crusade of the religious right to occupy the centers of power, and who accepted—indeed, eagerly sought—that ordination with no apparent sense of its internal irony or of its offensiveness to the Constitutional spirit.

The least that can be said of the legacy of that political misalliance is that it has left the American society with what the late Harvard historian Crane Brinton called the *odium theologicum*, "that intensest of hates—far more intense than the hate that springs from our simple lusts." Said Brinton, "At the very bottom in a democracy, most of us must really tolerate those who differ from us on [the] profound questions of man's fate." And that is precisely what fundamentalists have adamantly refused to do. Reagan gave presidential endorsement to that refusal when he told the prayer breakfast in Dallas that the religious among our citizens are the source of social tolerance, whereas the non-religious are the source of intolerance. It was taken up in even more theologically odious fashion by the former president of the Southern Baptist Convention, who declared that God does not hear the prayers of a Jew: and in a politically odious style by Pat Robertson, who asserted that only born-again Christians and devout Jews are worthy of appointment to public office. Said Jimmy Swaggart about the man who founded "People of the American Way," an organization designed to counter fundamentalist influence on public issues, "Norman Lear . . . is an atheistic Jew. There's nothing in the world any greater than to be a Jew, and nothing in the world any worse than being an atheistic Jew." In response, Lear's Lutheran friend, Martin Marty, wrote that Swaggart's charge is not merely intolerant; it is false.

> [Swaggart and Lear's other fundamentalist detractors] will most certainly hear from me . . . if they keep feeding the media charges that Lear is an atheist, with all that they want that epithet to connote. If they think that I think Lear is an orthodox theist, they have misread this. But if they henceforth portray him as an atheist who, in their terms, is beyond the bounds of civil discourse and moral inquiry, who does not respond to the stirrings we associate with *Theos*, I will know something about them. They may still have faith, but not good

faith. They will then continue to bear false witness against their neighbor. That remains a sin as gross as any of which they accuse him.[4]

The least that can be said of this misalliance between right-wing politicians and preachers—and in this case, the least is about as bad as the worst—is that they appear to be intent on closing the open society, ironically in the name of "true Americanism," as subsequent sections in this chapter will detail.

To anyone who finds such tactics dangerous to the wholeness of the American social fabric, as I do, the most hopeful thing to be said is that flaws that are inherent within the fundamentalist movement itself inevitably compromise its capacity for the kind of sustained political action on a national level that would be required to achieve its intent. However fundamentalism may succeed here and there in local political contests, largely because of doggedness and superior local organization, it is incapable of the long-term national unity that would be required to bring about that alteration in democratic political institutions it seems so devoutly to desire. It is the purpose of what follows in this chapter to assess the nature of that danger and to identify the flaws that are its mitigating hope.

MISREADING AMERICAN HISTORY

Fundamentalist leaders must have learned their American history in the same school system once described by Mark Twain. "I had a fine education," he said. "The only trouble was that so much of it wasn't so." That describes the way fundamentalists interpret the American experience: The trouble is that so much of that interpretation just isn't so, and it discloses an intellectual dishonesty and a disturbing ethical thrust that calls the whole fundamentalist argument into question.

Some might prefer, more charitably, to charge intellectual carelessness or historical ignorance; but I can think of no excuse for those who present themselves as the only true guardians of the American tradition not knowing the truth and speaking the truth about what they profess to guard.

Consider an example from Jerry Falwell, echoed throughout fundamentalism and the entire political right. Much is made of the contention that this nation was founded not as a democracy but as a republic. In *Listen America!* Falwell wrote, "Our Founding Fathers would not accept *the tyranny of a democracy* because they recognized that the only sovereign over men and nations was Almighty God" [emphasis added]. There is, of course, some validity in the distinction between "republic" and "democracy," in the sense that the founders provided for a president to be elected not directly by the people but by an Electoral College, and for matters of public policy to be decided not by popular referendum but by a representative legislature. And it is also true that America's founders frequently invoked, in their writings, a Creator who is the source of the natural and moral order.

But the Creator in eighteenth-century deism, who, having established that order, does not interfere in its operations, is scarcely the activist deity invoked by fundamentalism; nor does the narrowly sectarian America of fundamentalist interpretation at all resemble the broadly religious commonwealth envisioned by the founders. Similarly there is little resemblance between the "republican" intent of the Constitution's framers and the distinction between "republic" and "democracy" that is so precious to fundamentalism. To the fundamentalist's univocal aspirations, "democracy" carries too large an implication of ideological pluralism. The fundamentalist Baptist pastor who said, when reminded that the majority of Americans favor elective abortion, "This is still a republic; the majority isn't always right," clearly reflected fundamentalism's connection of republicanism with theocratic politics. The notion of a nation governed by the *vox populi* is too humanistic for the fundamentalist, who would like to have historical warrant for ignoring, or indeed for locking out of the political process, those who do not share fundamentalism's religiopolitical sensibilities.

An alarming example of such an attempted lockout is

found in the activities of the National Association of Christian Educators, a group dedicated to grass-roots organization of fundamentalist parents to take control of the public schools. In an NACE newsletter its president, Robert Simonds, wrote:

> We are small, we are weak, we are few and we are financially poor, but we are winning everywhere. We are now in the process of putting born-again Christians on every school board in America. How? by "COMMUNITY IMPACT EVANGELISM!" A school board with five members needs only three Christians to take complete control of a school district. You can literally own that system and control all personnel, curriculum, materials, textbooks, and policies. You will influence the "mindset" of between 20 and 50,000 children. It is worth it? All reasonable people would have to say "YES."[5]

Whatever warrant "born-again" Christians think they have for conspiring to take over the "ownership" of America's public schools, destroying the pluralistic character of those schools, turning them into agencies for the inculcation of a fundamentalist "mindset," and thereby making nonfundamentalist children aliens in their own land, that warrant cannot be located in the nation's founding. Any effort to turn the founders into theocratic enemies of ideological pluralism and of inclusive government is a distortion, willful or ignorant, and dangerous in either case; it is a distortion rooted in the desire of fundamentalists to claim that their religiopolitical views ought to be embraced by all loyal Americans because those views conform to the nation's founding intent.

The facts, I believe, are otherwise. In 1765, John Adams wrote that the motivation that created America "was not religion alone, as is commonly supposed." It was also "the love of universal liberty, and a hatred, a dread, a horror" of the "confederacy of temporal and spiritual tyranny" that characterized the reign of the House of Stuart in England. In other words, America was founded, by Adams's account, out of humanistic yearnings for freedom from ideological conformity and in abhorence of single-minded theocratic politics.

When Thomas Jefferson introduced in the Virginia legislature a bill to guarantee religious freedom, he made unmistakably clear his own preference for a pluralistic society in which political qualification bore no relation whatever to ideological profession. He wrote:

> Our civil rights have no dependence on our religious opinions, any more than our opinions in physics and geometry; therefore the proscribing of any citizen as unworthy of the public confidence by laying upon him an incapacity of being called to office of public trust . . . unless he profess or renounce this or that religious opinion, is depriving him injuriously of those privileges and advantages to which he has a natural [note the term] right.[6]

Clearly, Jefferson would have found the activities of the National Association of Christian Educators abhorrent.

As President, Jefferson was asked by a church association to declare an annual religious day of Thanksgiving. In rejecting that petition, he affirmed instead the constitutional principle of separation of church and state with respect to the observances of any religious body:

> Adhering to *this expression of the supreme will of the nation* [note that, for Jefferson, that supreme will resided in the Constitution and not in the divine sovereignty] in behalf of *the rights of conscience* [a notion derived from both religious and secular humanism], I shall see with sincere satisfaction the progress of those sentiments which tend to restore to man all his *natural rights* [a clear statement of eighteenth-century humanism], convinced that he had no natural right in opposition to his social duties [emphases added].[7]

James Madison shared Jefferson's conviction that political institutions have no business promoting or endorsing sectarian practices. So far was Madison from believing that the national legislature had need of an official chaplain for spiritual invocation and guidance, that he held such chaplaincy to be "a palpable violation of equal rights as well as of Constitutional principles." Said Madison, in words that bear not only on congressional chaplains paid out of the public treasury but equally on any effort to create an official piety, including school prayer:

> If religion consists in voluntary acts of individuals, singly or voluntarily associated, and if it be proper that public functionaries, as well as their constituents, should discharge their religious duties, let them, like their constituents, do so at their own expense.[8]

William Lee Miller, who has made a special study of the role of religion in the nation's founding, summarized the conclusion of that study in these striking words:

> Did "religious freedom" for Jefferson and Madison extend to atheists? Yes. To agnostics, unbelievers, and pagans? Yes. To heretics and blasphemers and the sacrilegious? Yes. To "the Jew and the Gentile, the Christian and the Mohametan, the Hindoo, and infidel of every denomination?" Yes. To Papists? Yes. To "irreligion"? Yes. To people who want freedom *from* religion? Yes. To people who want freedom *against* religion? Yes.[9]

Fundamentalist reading, or misreading, of American history notwithstanding, the Founding Fathers in the persons of Adams, Madison, and Jefferson were not the nation's founding fundamentalists. Indeed, if Jefferson were alive today, he would be denounced by Jerry Falwell as a liberal apostate. Jefferson's regard for the Hebrew-Christian scriptures was so selective and so contrary to fundamentalist notions of scripture's plenary authority that it permitted him to choose some portions and to reject others, finally creating and publishing a distinctive Jefferson Bible. Martin Marty describes Jefferson as "militant against orthodoxy" and pictures him spending "evenings cutting and pasting moral and non-miraculous elements of the Gospels together in a multilingual *The Life and Morals of Jesus of Nazareth*—while in the White House!"

A particularly dangerous form of historical ignorance or dishonesty is exhibited in fundamentalist knee-jerk invocations of the Monroe Doctrine in response to every hemispheric crisis, from the Cuban missiles to the Sandinistas, as if nothing has happened in the world since 1823. As a matter of fact, when President James Monroe sent his historic message to the Congress on December 2 of that year, it contained not one but two mutually entailed statements of policy: The first was a warning to European powers not to attempt to propagate their influence in the Western hemisphere; the other was an announcement that the United States intended to follow the advice of President Washington by avoiding foreign entanglements and would not interfere in the political affairs of Europe. How much sense does it make, historically, to appeal to the Monroe Doctrine, then, when American troops still occupy West Germany and American generals command the North Atlantic Treaty Organization, to say nothing of direct and indirect American entanglements in Asia, Africa, and the Middle East?

For a movement that wants to return America to its "traditions," this consistent fudging on historical issues is especially ironic. It betrays the disabling weakness in fundamentalist policy views that they can be argued only by resort to palpable distortion and dishonesty.

HOSTILITY TO AMERICAN TRADITIONS

One of the reasons why fundamentalists are unwilling or unable to come to terms with the American experience and feel free to offer it in distorted version is that, contrary to their public professions, they are basically hostile to many of its traditional features and want to see them radically altered.

Consider, for example, the impartiality of the judiciary on which justice based on laws rather than on men depends. The effort by Jerry Falwell and the Moral Majority to persuade the Reagan administration to impose an antiabortion test on candidates for appointment to the federal bench was a blatant attempt to create ideological conformity within the courts and to determine their decisions on specific issues in advance of a judicial and evidential hearing on those issues.

Consider the constitutional separation of powers, designed by the founders to prevent any of the three branches of government from subordinating the other two. Senator

Jesse Helms, perhaps fundamentalism's chief champion in the Congress, sponsored a bill to prohibit the federal courts from ever hearing any case involving public school activities that might be thought to be in violation of the "establishment of religion" clause of the Constitution—school prayer, for example, or the use of school facilities for religious purposes. Representative Les AuCoin of Oregon pointed to the constitutionally hostile implication of the Helms bill: "If Congress can throw up obstacles to subvert constitutional principles in matters of religion, then it can do the same thing when constitutional protections involving freedom of speech or assembly are at stake."

When Ronald Reagan, fundamentalism's president, charged that, in declaring school prayer unconstitutional, the Supreme Court had locked God and prayer out of the classroom, he surely should have known he was speaking blatant falsehood, not to say theological nonsense. Nothing in the Court's decision prohibited, nor in principle could have prohibited, the raising by any child or teacher of a private petition to God in the midst of school activities; and, since the Spirit "listeth where it will," no human power can exclude God where God wills to be present. Yet such presidential description had the effect of weakening the Court's legal and moral authority and of undermining its ability to win public confidence in its decisions. It fed the fundamentalist campaign for changes that would alter the traditional separation of powers and compromise the original ideal of ideological pluralism, thus subverting the "traditional" values fundamentalists profess to protect.

We may easily forget that what more recently became a campaign to permit a moment of silent meditation at the beginning of each school day began as a fundamentalist effort to permit the use of officially composed prayers in the classroom; nor may we doubt that, given the proper political climate, fundamentalists would return to their original sectarian intent.

Even more ominously (though when it comes to constitutional mischief making, it is difficult to decide what is more or less ominous), Reagan's (and fundamentalism's favorite) attorney general, Edwin Meese III, declared that, while persons who are innocent of a crime should have the right to an attorney when police question them, "the thing is, you don't have many suspects who are innocent of a crime. That's contradictory. If a person is innocent of a crime, then he is not a suspect." If that view were to prevail, the constitutional presumption of innocence, which is the cornerstone of our judicial system, would be replaced by a presumption of guilt. Said Harvard law professor Laurence Tribe, "Mere accusation does not transform one into a criminal. Civilized society could not long survive if Mr. Meese's views became prevalent."

Later the then-attorney general, further reflecting a distorted view of constitutional protections—one that is widely held among the religious and political right—asserted that the Miranda ruling, requiring police to notify a suspect of his rights before he is questioned, "flies in the face of constitutional government" and permits criminals to escape prosecution. Said Meese with astonishing candor, "Overturning Miranda would . . . be among the most important achievements of this administration."* Editorial response in *The Seattle Times* was headed "Aw C'mon, Ed!" and said that Meese,

> never a friend of civil libertarians, has outdone himself. . . .
> What baloney! Criminals don't escape prosecution because of Miranda, unless there's gross police error. And what timing! [Meese's Miranda view] comes just as the country is preparing to celebrate the bicentennial of the . . . Constitution—a document with which Miranda is in perfect harmony.[10]

Clearly, a fundamentalist America would *not* be the America of our traditions.

---

*In a 1988 book, Terrel Bell, Reagan's first secretary of education, depicts Meese as "a man who literally detested the federal government," and said Meese led a group of "movement conservatives" (i.e., political fundamentalists) who operated almost like a secret society to steer administration policies to the right.

LACK OF CREDIBILITY WITH CONSERVATIVES

With the exception of a school board or other local office here and there, direct political power, in contrast to political influence, has eluded fundamentalists to date. If they were to increase their influence and turn it into real power, they would have to forge a stable alliance with conservatives who already have power and who can give the fundamentalist persona and agenda the broader credibility they need but have been unable to generate out of their own intellectual and political resources.

Unfortunately for them, and fortunately for the rest of us, it is precisely the prospect of ideological subversion, which we have just been examining, that regularly costs fundamentalists the support of religious and political conservatives. On the surface the two appear to have much in common politically: a professed desire to reduce the interference of government in the lives of its citizens, a commitment to a strong military establishment, a militant anti-Soviet stance, a hard-line approach to law-and-order issues, a repudiation of the social experiments conducted by the government since the 1930s, the call for a return to "traditional" values, and so on. In spite of appearances, however, there is no direct connection between the two groups. Sometimes, to be sure, a fundamentalist is merely a conservative gone sour; but one can become a fundamentalist without ever having passed through conservatism. That there are people on the far right, whose previous political home was on the far left, and who have moved from one extremity to the other with no intermediate stops, should not surprise us, given the similarities in those extremes noted in chapter 1.

What motivates conservatives is a set of coherent social and political principles and a commitment to translate that principled vision into institutional and personal life-styles. In contrast, what motivates fundamentalists is frustration and outrage that history has not moved in their desired direction and at their command. Having no coherent intellectual vision of their own and often displaying a virulently antiintellectual cast, fundamentalists appropriate elements from the conservative agenda because they lack the capacity to create their own intellectual armament; which is to say that that appropriation is not so much principled as it is weaponed. Fundamentalism is a kind of rampant nostalgia that clings desperately to nonthreatening patterns in a world that grows daily more threatening. Unfortunately, the "past" to which fundamentalism appeals is not what it used to be; for, as has already been seen, that appeal is not to the past as it was but as the fundamentalists wish it had been.

Frustration, outrage, desperation, and latent violence (hear it in fundamentalist denunciations of "secular humanists," homosexuals, Roman Catholics, Mormons, and supporters of abortion rights, among others) are the motive forces in fundamentalist behavior, and they lead inevitably to behavioral unpredictability, opportunism, and recklessness. All of this is profoundly embarrassing to many conservatives, who are likely to think of fundamentalists as a bunch of crazies giving a bad name to some good causes.

The Family Protection Act, put together by a group of religious and political fundamentalists and introduced in Congress in 1978 by Senator Paul Laxalt, so alarmed the conservative columnist James J. Kilpatrick that he wrote:

> [If this is a conservative measure, then] I have wasted my adult life in understanding and promoting conservative causes. This bill is a hodgepodge of good intentions and bad law. . . . The sponsors of this misbegotten bill would involve "recognized religious groups" in decisions relating to [public school] courses that touch on religious beliefs. They would require "parental review" of text books prior to adoption. They would intrude upon the right and power of the states to fix certification requirements for teachers. They would snatch funds from any state that prohibited "voluntary prayer" on the premises of any public building.
>
> What in the world, may we gently inquire, has become of the conservative's traditional dedication to states' rights? What of the wall that conservatives insist should be maintained between church and state? . . . The bill is hopeless. It attempts to cover everything under moon or sun. . . . In one way or another, the bill violates just about every precept of a con-

servative political philosophy. Legislatively speaking, it is so much junk. It ought to be quietly scrapped.[11]

In the fall of 1986, a federal district judge held that the "free exercise of religion" of a group of fundamentalist parents in Tennessee had been "burdened" by the exposure of their children to classroom literature that was at odds with the parents' religious beliefs. Readings at issue included *The Diary of Anne Frank, The Wizard of Oz*, the story of Cinderella, Shakespeare's *MacBeth*, and the stories of Hans Christian Andersen, among others. Said the judge, "The plaintiffs have sincerely held beliefs which are entitled to protection under the law."

"Hold it," wrote conservative columnist George Will in commenting on the decision.

> Constitutional protection of belief? Protection from what? Literature? Science? The 20th century? The free exercise clause . . . is not a guarantee of intellectual or spiritual serenity, or a commitment to protect parents and children from influences that might complicate the transmission of sectarian beliefs.[12]

The pluralistic society that was intended at the nation's founding depends, said the conservative Will,

> on tolerance of diversity, a value subverted by assertion of a constitutional right to retreat from all but comforting instruction. Furthermore, there is a social interest not only in pluralism but in commonality, a shared grammar of the intellect. . . . [And he concluded,] If a court holds that bad teaching is unconstitutional, conservative judicial activism will have produced a judicial supervision of American life far more intrusive than anything liberal activism has achieved.[13]

Senator Barry Goldwater, widely known as "Mr. Conservative" ever since his 1964 presidential bid, complained in a 1981 speech about fundamentalist presumption and the arrogance and invidiousness of fundamentalist tactics. The Moral Majority and other "pro-life" and religious groups may be called "the new conservatism," said Goldwater, "but I can say with conviction that the religious issues of these groups have little or nothing to do with conservative or liberal politics." The senator affirmed his own commitment to traditional "morality, family closeness, self-reliance, and a day's pay for a day's work" and expressed pleasure "with the swing of the pendulum in recent years" toward these issues. "But," he said, "I object to certain groups jumping on that pendulum, and then claiming that they caused it to swing in the first place."

Goldwater also took issue with "the uncompromising positions of these groups [which] is a divisive element that could tear apart the very spirit of our representative system, if they gain sufficient strength." He was "sick and tired," he said, of having political preachers tell him what he has to believe if he wants to be a moral person. "Just who do they think they are?" he asked in apparent high dudgeon. "I am warning them today: I will fight them every step of the way if they try to dictate their moral convictions to all Americans in the name of 'conservatism.'"

It seems clear, from these and other pieces of evidence that could be adduced, that there is no foreseeable prospect of a stable coalition between conservatives, such as Kilpatrick, Will, and Goldwater, and militant fundamentalists, for at least two reasons: The first is that the fundamentalist tactic is antithetical to stability and thus abhorrent to the conservative temper. Said Howard Phillips, head of the new-right Conservative Caucus, "We organize discontent." And said Paul Weyrich, director of the new-right Committee for the Survival of a Free Congress, "We are different from previous generations of conservatism. We are no longer working to preserve the status quo. We are radicals, working to overturn the present power structure in this country."

The second reason is that the fundamentalist character makes for very unpredictable partnership. That character is *paranoid* (John Birch founder Robert Welch was its prototype, with his charge that President Eisenhower was "a conscious agent of the Communist conspiracy"); *opportunistic* (prepared to make any issue a test of "conservatism" and "morality" if it promises political leverage); *impulsive* (recall Jerry Falwell's characterization of Bishop Desmond Tutu as a "phony," a comment he and others in the movement lived to regret); and *reactionary* (Falwell has been an apologist for South Africa's apartheid government, Swaggart has been a supporter of Chilean dictator Augusto Pinochet, and Robertson has been an ally of Guatemalan strongman General José Efraín Rios Montt, raising even more serious questions about their devotion to "traditional" American political values).

Not even the need for electoral power positioning is likely to be strong enough to compel establishment conservatives to pour themselves into this kind of oil-and-water political brew.

A SEPARATIST TEMPER

Anyone who has studied the dynamics of American fundamentalism knows that it has a history of schism. While as a result of the ecumenical movement, the number of mainline Protestant bodies has decreased markedly through merger over the last fifty years, fundamentalist bodies and individual splinter congregations have proliferated. The reason is fairly simple. Each fundamentalist leader traces his own peculiar views to divine revelation, which means that those views are believed to carry the authority of God. The difficulty is that fundamentalist leaders often disagree with one another's interpretations of what is divinely revealed. Some, for example, hold that the second coming of Christ will occur at the beginning of a final worldwide Tribulation, some that it will occur at the end, and still others that it will occur at its mid-point. Some fundamentalists believe that speaking in tongues under the influence of the Holy Spirit ended with the conclusion of the apostlic period and that any such contemporary phenomenon is the work of the devil; others believe as passionately that God continues to possess his chosen agents in that way today.

Obviously each party cannot be correct, but given the putative source of its belief—in a divinely inspired and inerrant scripture or in the immediacy of the indwelling Spirit—no one is willing to yield, believing that to do so would be contrary to God's word and will. When such differences arise, therefore, the only course is the separation of "believer" from "unbeliever," as fundamentalists are convinced the New Testament requires.

Hence, schism multiplied hundreds of times across the face of American fundamentalism, often on issues that may seem trivial, at best, to the rest of us; but to fundamentalists, nothing is trivial as they believe it to be commanded by God.

The far right in this country is an unstable and tenuous collection, made up of those who, politically nouveau riche thanks to the climate generated in the Reagan years, had experienced virtual disenfranchisement during a fifty-year period prior to 1980 as a result of "liberal" control (actually, control by a coalition of establishment conservatives and establishment liberals) of the two major political parties, and of the mainline Protestant denominational bureaucracies and their seminaries. On its religious side the collection includes charismatics and Pentecostals, faith healers and theological scholastics, pre- and post-Tribulationists, some Mormons and Roman Catholics, ecclesiastics, sectarians, and assorted independent free lancers, to cite only a few. On its political side, it includes militant isolationists and militant interventionists, antiabortionists, antifeminists, antigays, libertarians, trade protectionists, capital-punishment friends and income-tax foes, again to cite only a few, some of whom are single-issue advocates. And it is made up of those whose primary claim is to a faith motivation, as well as those whose motivation is primarily political (sometimes called "movement conservatives" but whom I prefer to denominate "political fundamentalists" to avoid any confusion with mainline conservatives like Goldwater, Kilpatrick, and Will).

There is no common intellectual or social vision that binds this strange mix to a common political destiny. Thirty years ago evangelical theologian Edward J. Carnell complained that fundamentalism has "no unifying principle." "Content," as Carnell said, "with the single virtue of negating modernism" and "no longer in union with the wisdom of the ages," it became merely "a religious mentality" whose "status [is maintained] by negation." Carnell's 1958 characterization is echoed in the much more recent comment by political fundamentalist Howard Phillips: "We organize discontent." And political fundamentalist Paul Weyrich identified the single item on the common agenda: "We are radicals, working to overturn the . . . power structure" that has ruled this country since the days of Franklin Roosevelt, through both Democratic and Republican administrations, right up to the moment of Ronald Reagan.

Even in the case of fundamentalism's president, which Reagan clearly was, there was enormous disappointment and renewed anger within the right after January of 1981 that so few true believers were appointed to positions of real power in his administration, in spite of the fact that his winning was in part due to enthusiastic endorsement and activism by religious and political fundamentalists. As usual for that "Teflon" president, responsibility for the betrayal was assigned elsewhere, as often as not to the malign influence of the more "liberal" members of the White House staff. Worse, some of the rightists who did make it into important positions—James Watt at Interior, Jeane Kirkpatrick at the United Nations, Richard Allen at the National Security Council, Ann Burford at the Environmental Protection Agency—left the administration under a variety of circumstances well before its terms were over. At least one promotion important to fundamentalism—that of William Bradford Reynolds to be associate attorney general—was headed off at the pass by the Senate's "liberal" establishment.

So an adhesive discontent, fueled by an optimism that, in spite of some relatively minor reverses, American political momentum might at last be moving in fundamentalism's direction and that larger gains of influence and power might lie just ahead, held this precarious collection together. Optimistic discontent—and Ronald Reagan. Given fundamentalism's authoritarian character, it succumbs regularly and readily to the cult of personality. For Protestant fundamentalists, the Bible is the professed source of authority for faith and life. The difficulty is that the Bible does not interpret itself authoritatively. Given the symbolic and poetic nature of much that it contains and its consequent opaqueness for even the most devout general reader, an authoritative Bible requires an authoritative interpreter, presumably gifted and authorized by the Holy Spirit, who can read its signs and penetrate its mysteries for the saving edification of ordinary believers not gifted with that kind of putative insight. So the leader is the essence of the movement—shapes its persona, gives it legitimation, infuses it with his own rhetorical power.

This is the significance of the following that gathers around such television personalities as Oral Roberts, Jimmy Swaggart, Jerry Falwell, Kenneth Copeland, Pat Robertson. For such audiences, coherence comes not from a common creedal confession, as in the Reformed churches, nor from a prayer book, as in the Anglican Communion, nor from a history of witness, as among Friends—not even from the Bible itself, given the uninterpreted confusion of its voices. What provides coherence is the spirit-filled interpreter, who can tell the faithful authoritatively just how things are in the mind of God. Jerry Falwell once justified his own authoritarian role this way:

> God never intended for a committee nor a board of deacons nor any other group to dominate a church or control a pastor. The pastor is God's man, God's servant, God's leader. When you tie the hands of God's man, when you keep him from acting as the Holy Spirit leads him, you have murdered his initiative, you have killed his spirit.[14]

The fact that "spirit-led" interpreters like Falwell do not agree among themselves is, as has been seen, the major factor contributing to fundamentalism as a history of schism.

In the past, the main condition contributing to fundamentalism's political weakness and ineptitude—whether the politics be ecclesiastical or civil—has been its under-dog mentality, in which it seems that, however unfair the rules had been made by the "power elite," there was little or nothing that could be done to change them, with the result that fulmination was the only available retaliatory weapon. This earlier powerlessness and its resultant divisiveness were further complicated by the absence of an authoritative national leader, who could focus anger and discontent, give it voice and vector, and transcend inherent differences in a working unity. For a time it looked as if Billy Graham might be such a leader, but mutual disenchantment—Graham with the extremists in the movement and the movement with Graham—eliminated that possibility. So, under the circumstances of powerlessness and national leaderlessness, fundamentalists focused all their energy and attention on the things that divided them, engaged in spiritual civil war, fulminating against one another as well as against the external enemy, since invidiousness was the only power they knew.

The period of Ronald Reagan's ascendancy was not such a time. In those years, fundamentalists became upbeat and aggressive, because for the first time in American history they found themselves with a charismatic champion, himself a man of power in whom they experienced power vicariously, who was able to give eloquence and political promise to their discontent. In such circumstance, they could sublimate their otherwise fractious differences for the sake of an unsurpassed, indeed scarcely dreamed of, prospect of overturning more than a half century of what they considered to be political and religious apostasy and of "returning" America to its "true" faith.

What long-term leverage are the fundamentalists likely to extract from the advantage the 1980s have given them? Considering the character of the movement, my prediction is that they will snatch defeat from the jaws of victory, partly in spite of and partly because of the enormous boost they experienced in those years, a prediction that is based on two considerations.

The first is the consequence that has followed from the transition of Ronald Reagan from charismatic leader, capable of galvanizing fundamentalist political energies and of transcending the movement's inherent divisiveness, to elder statesman, whose magic is dissipated by his loss of direct political power. In spite of the fact that it had achieved substantially greater strength by the end of the Reagan era than it had at its beginning, fundamentalism is unlikely to sustain that strength for very long in this new, post-Reagan era of American politics. Sidney Blumenthal, writing in *The Washington Post*, shares my view of that unlikelihood: "The greatest organizing principle for conservatives for more than a generation has been Reagan. But when movement conservatism is disconnected from his pleasing image, its internal contradictions may flare into factional warfare. Without the benefit of Reagan's mediating persona . . . accommodations [among the movements diverse factions could collapse]."

Not only could collapse; in my view, will collapse, for reasons that are religious even more than political. While there are, among fundamentalism's religious luminaries, potential candidates for its national leadership, none gives promise of being able to match Reagan's unifying, galvanic appeal. Unlike Reagan, whose shadowy spirituality served remarkably to unify the movement in part because it was impossible to tar him with any sectarian brush, the only truly national figures who might press fundamentalism's full politico-religious agenda are themselves unmistakable sectarians, capable of arousing as much controversy and disaffection within the movement as they do outside of it.

Jerry Falwell earned the enmity of Pentecostals because of his blunt hostility to speaking in tongues and his brief tenure as Pentecostal Jim Bakker's successor in turning Bakker's former PTL (Praise the Lord) ministry away from its Pentecostal ethos.

Pat Robertson, a Pentecostal in practice though not in denomination, scandalizes biblicist fundamentalists of the Falwell stripe because of his reports of conversations with God. (According to Robertson, God once told him, "Pat, I want you to have an RCA transmitter".) He alienated many Pentecostals because of his charge, in a 1988 "authorized" biography, that former colleague Jim Bakker was guilty of financial irregularities during the years when Bakker was Robertson's closest associate in the Christian Broadcasting Network. But in his 1972 autobiography, Robertson had sung Bakker's praises and cited Bakker's faith healing before

Robertson's "700 Club" cameras as evidence of Bakker's deep spirituality. Pentecostals have not been the only ones to wonder why, if Robertson knew that Bakker had been involved in shady financial practices, he had been so lavish in his praise of the younger man until Robertson's political ambition made his earlier friendship with Bakker, who had become the subject of a sex scandal, a liability. Robertson's political ambitions have been opposed by many on the religious right out of fear that what conservative journalist John McLaughlin called Robertson's "wacko factor"—his claim of conversations with God, of faith healing, of miraculous intervention with hurricanes—may bring the entire movement into public disrepute. In a 1987 preferential poll of National Association of Evangelicals board members, Robertson placed fourth among Republican presidential nomination contenders, garnering only 17 percent of the board's vote. Maverick evangelist Gene Scott, the bearded, cigar-smoking eccentric who always wears a hat on his television programs and has been openly critical of his fellow evangelists, said of Pat Robertson, "His first name almost exhausts the subject."

Jimmy Swaggart, who was commonly considered to be the most powerful of the television evangelists because he had attracted the largest television audience, has been perhaps the most sectarian of all the movement's luminaries. In addition to his Pentecostalism, he has openly characterized Roman Catholicism as a "false religion." His spectacular fall from grace in the 1988 scandal involving his liaison with a New Orleans prostitute effectively destroyed any national political influence he might have had.

Nor are candidates to carry on a Reaganesque leadership of the movement to be found within the political arena from which Reagan came. In spite of efforts by some Republican politicians to pander to fundamentalist interests and to seek fundamentalist support, none has demonstrated the double requisite of piety and national political charisma to carry the movement beyond the place where Reagan left it.

The second consideration is that fundamentalists are likely to snatch defeat from the jaws of victory not only in spite of the strengths gained in the 1980s, as I have just been arguing, but precisely because of that strength. The one condition that, ironically, can return the movement to the state of schism leading to weakness and ineptitude—the condition in which it languished during earlier decades of this century—is precisely the prospect of success. Once having achieved, or even being on the verge of achieving, the influence bordering on real power so long denied to them, and faced with the opportunity to jockey for position within the new order they think may be about to dawn, the temptation again to be themselves—that is, to luxuriate in the invidiousness that is endemic to fundamentalism—will be all but irresistible. They exercised that luxury with abandon during the long years when power was out of the question. The sweet smell of success has the effect of freeing them again to turn against one another. Indeed, it will virtually compel them to do so since, as has already been seen, each leader believes that his differences from the others, whether in politics or in religion, have no casual human source but can be traced to the mind of God. Such a confrontation would be all but irresolvable. Says former fundamentalist Timothy Sims, "A debate among a Bob Jones type, a hardshell Baptist, a Wisconsin-Synod Lutheran, a Seventh-Day Adventist, and Jimmy Swaggart about the meaning of Revelation 12 would be like Milton's hell, where fallen angels debate theology 'in wandering mazes lost.' "

In fact, just such a series of divisive confrontations began in the spring of 1987, for reasons that appeared less principled than disagreement over whether or not one had received a direct, God-given revelation. The media called it "the holy wars"—conflict among some of the leading television evangelists that surfaced with the Jim Bakker scandal involving his sexual dalliance with a church secretary and then-unsubstantiated allegations of homosexual liaisons. The conflict ostensibly centered in moral revulsion but seemed to have as much to do with internecine rivalry and jealousy among the evangelist empire builders as anything else. The Pentecostal Jim Bakker turned control of his PTL ministry over to the biblicist Jerry Falwell because, by Bakker's own account, a "hostile takeover" of PTL was being engineered by his fellow-Pentecostal Jimmy Swaggart, who had brought Bakker's sexual misadventure to the attention of Assemblies of God officials. Fundamentalism was so ripe with heretofore-sublimated rivalries that it was only a matter of hours before the television preachers began to choose sides and to accuse one another in the Bakker controversy, drawing in to its maelstrom Falwell, Swaggart, Oral Roberts, Pat Robertson, and John Ankerberg, among others, and threatening to leave no one untouched by its intramural animus and by the public disrepute in which it seemed to cast the entire evangelistic enterprise.

Then, ironically, charges of sexual misconduct were leveled against Jimmy Swaggart early in 1988 by his fellow-Pentecostal Marvin Gorman, leading to a formal censure of Swaggart by the Assemblies of God from which both men derived their ordination. It was apparently a "turn-about-is-fair-play" scenario, for Swaggart had earlier charged Gorman with multiple sexual affairs, with the result that Gorman had been defrocked by the denomination. All of which demonstrates how fragile—emotionally as well as religiously—the fundamentalist coalition is.

A CENTRIST TENDENCY

There were less sensational signs of collapsing unity within the movement even before those affairs erupted. In 1985, the *Washington Post* reported that Jerry Falwell was "moving deliberately to take the hard edge off his public image and [reaching] out to a broader American audience." Reporter Kathy Sawyer wrote that

> Falwell has softened his position on abortion to "get some-thing through" the Congress, says he considers his former nemesis George Bush a fine presumptive heir to President Reagan, is contemplating a massive mobilization of the faithful to send food and medicine to the starving in Marxist-led Ethiopia and is calling on church people to do more to help the poor. He is even promising to "liberate" fundamentalist women in 1985.[15]

Even more remarkable was an incident reported by Rabbi

Marc Tanenbaum in a 1985 letter to *Time* magazine, which said in part:

> In March I publicly debated [the] issue of a Christian America with Jerry Falwell. After I reminded him of [the historic] Baptist struggle on behalf of religious liberty [Falwell is a Baptist], he said, "I know I have been preaching the Christianization of America. I now realize that I was mistaken and I apologize to the Jewish community. We are not a Christian nation. We do not want a state church. This is a pluralistic society."[16]

The rabbi properly noted that "Mr. Falwell's statement is an important clarification of his unfolding Fundamentalist theology, and it ought not be lost in the historical record." Such "unfolding" of Falwell's theology had assuredly not been lost on some of his fellow fundamentalists, and he had been roundly denounced for his pains. Bob Jones, president of Bob Jones University, a fundamentalist enclave in South Carolina, called Falwell "the most dangerous man in America," whose political manipulations were "spiritual fornication." The Fundamentalist Baptist Association passed a resolution taking Falwell to task for substituting "moral reformation" for saving grace. Attempting to reform America's morals, as Falwell is doing, is merely "cosmetic," said the resolution; the real problem is sin.

In attempting to consolidate political gains won earlier in the 1980s, it was not surprising that a major fundamentalist leader should attempt to moderate his public image and with it the image of his movement. Cal Thomas, then an official of Falwell's Moral Majority, had said, "The first [Reagan] term earned us the right to be heard. In the second, we have to earn the right to be followed." Of all of the fundamentalist leaders in the 1980s, Falwell appeared to have the greatest access to governing politicians in Washington.* He,

---

*Not, however, as much as Falwell sometimes claimed. He once announced that he had been called by then-president Gerald Ford, who wanted to assure Falwell that he totally disagreed with the views of Jimmy Carter as reported in *Playboy*'s 1976 Carter interview. Falwell later admitted publicly that there had been no such call from Ford.

more than others, could therefore have been expected to understand that governing is almost always a matter of compromise and coalition. If, then, the influence already achieved by organizations like the Moral Majority were to be retained and extended, and if such groups were to enlarge their roles in actually governing the country, Falwell must have known that they would, indeed, have to "earn the right to be followed" by appealing to a larger segment of the voting public. And that would inevitably mean moderating the extremist rhetoric and substance of what had been the prevailing fundamentalist political agenda.

What was evident in Falwell's move toward moderation is an essential development in the life of any would-be-viable political movement. In the American system, there is an almost irresistible centrist tendency that draws those in power, and those who think they are seriously within reach of power, to a more mainstream position. Americans saw that in the contrast between the George Wallace presidential campaign of 1968, when he was merely a gadfly and could afford to be outrageous, and the Wallace campaign of 1972, a much more moderate affair because Wallace had concluded that, given wide public disenchantment with both Richard Nixon and Hubert Humphrey, he had at last a chance to become a serious national contender.

Not understanding the pull of this centrist tendency, and expecting President Reagan to make the right-wing decisions and to appoint the right-wing persons he had promised when he was merely Candidate Reagan, his fundamentalist followers were keenly disappointed when decisions and appointments were more moderate than they had permitted themselves to expect. The fact, as Reagan and others have repeatedly experienced it, is that once political power has been achieved, it can be retained only by consent of the governed in their varieties, only by consolidating power through the coopting of constituencies that may not have been sympathetic at an earlier stage but whose interests

---

There had been a call from a White House aide, who, however, had expressed no opinion on either Ford or the Carter interview.

must be addressed if their consent is to be won and kept. That is the price of being able to govern.

Pat Robertson is the George Wallace of the present political era, and his style has its direct analogue in the Wallace campaign of 1968. The appeal of both men has been strongest in the South and among hard-core, extreme-right, disenchanted voters elsewhere. Two things characterize the style Robertson shares with the 1968 Wallace, a style that falls like manna on his constituency: a reckless political opportunism that makes the most outrageous and baseless charges, in order to keep that constituency's anger and discontent fueled, its political adrenalin high, and his opponents off-balance; and a paranoia that cries "conspiracy" and "cover-up" when those charges are refuted. So, for example, in his bid for the 1988 Republican presidential nomination, Robertson announced that it is possible to contract AIDS simply by being in the same room with and breathing the same air as a group of persons already afflicted with the disease, and claimed that the medical and governmental establishment was deliberately keeping that grim "truth" from the American public. Later he charged that the Soviet Union had secretly placed twenty-five intermediate-range nuclear missiles in Cuba and that the Reagan administration had deliberately kept that information from the public in order to win congressional ratification of the Intermediate Nuclear Forces Treaty that had been signed earlier by President Reagan and Soviet General Secretary Mikhail Gorbachev. Denials from medical researchers and from the White House that either of these things was true seemed not to dent the candidate or daunt his followers.

When television news anchor Tom Brokaw referred to Robertson, in an interview, as a former television evangelist, Robertson testily charged Brokaw with "bigotry," arguing, in spite of Brokaw's entirely accurate characterization, that any invocation of Robertson's clerical past represented a conspiracy to deny him the presidential nomination on purely religious grounds. Perhaps most paranoid of all, Robertson declared that the public exposure of Jimmy Swaggart's sexual indiscretion, presumably brought about by fellow-evangelist Marvin Gorman in apparent revenge for Swaggart's earlier exposure of Gorman, was really a plot aimed at Robertson and designed to diminish his political fortunes in the Republican presidential primaries, apparently on the principle that to bring one television evangelist into disrepute is to bring a candidate who resists even being identified as a former television evangelist into disrepute. "Nothing happens to people by accident," Robertson told a reporter. "It's kind of funny this came up two weeks before the most important primaries in the nation. . . . Somebody else planned these things, I'm afraid." While declining to specify who that "somebody" might be, Robertson hinted broadly, in the same interview, that it was, in fact, Vice President George Bush, whom he accused of "dirty politics" and "trickery." For its part, the Bush campaign characterized Robertson's remarks as "bizarre."

If Robertson were to attempt a consolidation of the political gains achieved from his first bid for public office, he would have to follow the example of the 1972 George Wallace and begin a move toward the political center. For what is a general rule of American political behavior is even more critical in the case of the fundamentalist movement. The unstable coalition of the angry and discontented that has brought it this far would have to seek accommodation with more stable centers of influence if a larger electoral consent were to be won; and that would require a more reasoned and less invidious style, which is apparently just what Jerry Falwell had in mind.

If so, it may have been his undoing within the movement itself. In January 1986, in a further effort to distance himself from some of the more extreme posturing of the past and reach out to a wider constituency, especially in foreign policy matters, Falwell founded the Liberty Federation. But late in 1987, he suddenly announced his permanent retirement from direct political activism to return, full-time, to the pastorate of the Thomas Road Baptist Church in Lynchburg, Virginia. Falwell's experience may suggest that no fundamentalist-becoming-centrist can survive within fundamentalism's dog-eat-dog politics.

A HOPEFUL CONCLUSION

It is important to be clear that the fundamentalist phenomenon is not ominous because it mixes religion and politics. That is an altogether appropriate mix, politics having more need of principle against which to test its pragmatism than it usually gets from politicians, and religion having more need of situational specificity to test its hortatory and moralistic proclivities than it ordinarily gets from preachers.

What is ominous is the historical carelessness, the constitutional hostility, the unpredictability and extremity, and withal the ideological polarization that are among fundamentalism's chief characteristics.

And there is at least one other reason for deploring its baleful effect on political dialogue in this country—a reason supplied by historian Christopher Lasch:

> Adherents of the new religious right correctly reject the separation of religion and politics, but they bring no spiritual insights to politics. They campaign against pornography, but they have nothing to tell us about its roots in the larger consumerist structure of addiction-maintenance. They believe that the proper relation between politics and religion can be achieved simply by invoking religious sanctions for specific political positions, as when they declaim that budget deficits, progressive taxation, and the presence of women in the armed forces are "anti-biblical." The religiosity of the American right is self-righteous and idolatrous. It perceives no virtue in its opponents and magnifies its own.[17]

Yet the fact is that self-righteousness and arrogance generate energy and momentum, especially in politics. So what shall we say about their prospects? Shall the fundamentalists win?

Nonfundamentalists have worried, and fundamentalists have hoped, that the enormous audiences enjoyed by major television evangelists might translate into overwhelming electoral power. Yet the results of a 1987 *New York Times*/CBS News poll raised serious questions about so simple an equation. Even among those who regularly watched Jim Bakker, Jerry Falwell, Rex Humbard, Oral Roberts, Pat

Robertson, Jimmy Swaggart, and Robert Schuller, 50 percent reported coming away from that watching with an unfavorable opinion of what they had heard and seen; 37 percent reported a favorable opinion. Only 20 percent of regular viewers thought Robertson should run for President; 81 percent of those regular viewers said they did not believe Roberts when he said that God would "call him home" if he did not raise $8 million within a particular three-month period. One suspects that viewership permits us to draw conclusions about the perceived entertainment value of television evangelism but not about matters of political, or even of religious, substance.

For anyone who finds fundamentalist politics menacing, as I do, the conclusion to be drawn from the analysis in this chapter is a hopeful one, on five counts:

First, the aggressive and largely independent role of the press in the American political system means that individuals and movements are subjected to a searching examination, and the more serious the contention, the more pitiless the scrutiny. I doubt that fundamentalism's record of historical carelessness and dishonesty can avoid being thoroughly discredited in any campaign in which it essays a major role. Even the Reagan White House has had to mount continuous and frantic efforts at damage control in the aftermath of Reagan's repeated thoughtless comment and apparently deliberate misstatement. A lesser figure would long since have fatally wounded himself, as Gerald Ford did when, in debate with Jimmy Carter, he blundered into the comment that Eastern Europe was not under Soviet control. And fundamentalism offers only a choice of lesser figures.

Second, what will become increasingly and discreditingly clear from such scrutiny is that the fundamentalist appeal to "traditional American values" is a mask for its hostility toward some of our most basic political institutions, including judicial independence, constitutional liberties, social and religious pluralism, and the equal access to the political process that is promised to all citizens irrespective of ideology.

Third, the regular efforts that establishment conservatives

make to distance and distinguish themselves from fundamentalists, in spite of superficial resemblances, deprive fundamentalism of a critically important source of credibility
and influence. Lacking that, any more serious bid for political power will be virtually out of the question.

Fourth, even without conservative disenchantment, fundamentalism's political future is in trouble because it is full
of unpredictable, uncontrollable, centrifugal forces that,
with no substantial prospect either of achieving its aims or
of being entirely deprived of them, are likely to tear the
movement apart by the power of their own internal invidiousness.

Finally, fundamentalism cannot succeed in its political
ambition simply out of its own resources. Success would
require a willing and respectful alliance with constituencies
not presently a part of it or in sympathy with it. And having
established such an alliance, the resulting political accommodation would be unlikely to bear much resemblance to
the fundamentalist agenda.

The obverse implication of these five considerations is
clear: Fundamentalists can win through to their political
aims only if (1) they have the will to create a new intellectual
integrity and credibility, (2) they rededicate themselves to
America's basic political institutions, (3) they moderate their
erratic behavior to the satisfaction of establishment conservatives, (4) they can find the grace to tolerate ideological
differences within the movement itself, and (5) they become
pragmatic enough to make the accommodations required of
those who aspire to govern.

All of which is to say that, if the fundamentalists are to
have any prospect of long-term political success, they will
have to cease being fundamentalists!

CHAPTER 5

Fundamentalism and the Age to Come: History Before It Happens?

Is THE END OF THE WORLD NEAR? Does God intend to bring history to a violent close within our generation, perhaps within this very decade?

Twenty-five years ago, biblical scholar Thomas F. Kepler wrote in a popular commentary on Daniel and Revelation: "Should anyone today make minute predictions about events in world history between now and the year A.D. 2400, he would not be likely to have an audience. He would merely be labelled a fanatic."

Perhaps that observation demonstrates how radically and unpredictably the world has changed since 1963. For today preachers and Bible teachers all across the land are, indeed, making "minute predictions about events in world history." Moreover, they confidently claim to be discovering, among politicians and powers on the present world scene, the long-hidden identities of mysterious figures in certain biblical writings—especially Daniel and Ezekiel and Revelation—thus purporting to disclose the plan God has had for the history of our own time from the very beginning of creation. They are welcoming emergent events—wars and rumors of wars, technological advancements, and social tragedies—whether or not explicitly anticipated in those strange bibli-

cal writings, as confirmation that the decisive and cataclysmic intervention in the affairs of men promised by God
in biblical times may occur at any moment, indeed, *will*
occur in near-term history.

And rather than being dismissed as lunatic fringe, these
teachers of so-called prophecy have an audience that numbers in the millions.

The phenomenal public success of Hal Lindsey's books on
biblical prediction of the end times—*The Late Great Planet
Earth* (with C.C. Carlson) and *There's a New World Coming*
chief among them—led the *New York Times* to call him the
best-selling author of the decade. Lindsey is only one of a
number of fundamentalist authors who purport to bring
biblical illumination to the anxious uncertainty of our times;
others include Tim LaHaye (*The Beginning of the End, The
Coming Peace in the Middle East*), John F. Walvoord and
John E. Walvoord (*Armageddon, Oil and the Middle East
Crisis*), David Allen Lewis (*Magog 1982 Cancelled*), and
Herbert W. Armstrong (*The United States and British Commonwealth in Prophecy, Who Is the Beast?*). The most
widely watched television evangelists—Jerry Falwell, Rex
Humbard, Kenneth Copeland, Pat Robertson, and Oral
Roberts—have been earnestly and urgently warning their
followers that the end of history is near. And in large cities
and small, independent Bible teachers and fundamentalist
preachers of lesser note are growing increasingly bolder in
their claim to discern, accurately and with divine authorization, the portentous signs of the times.

One of the significant features of this current **apocalyptic**
mood, apart from the apparent size of the crowd that has
been drawn into it, is that fundamentalists do not appear to
be the only ones who are turning a serious ear to the purveyors of biblical "prophecy." Here and there, Christians of
other theological persuasion, along with troubled men and
women outside of the churches, are beginning to wonder
whether there may be something in it. I suspect this is partly
the result of the incessant repetition of the theme across the
television dial and partly because events themselves—the
doomsday nuclear policies that have been pursued by the

United States and the Soviet Union for thirty years and the dangerously-deepening crisis in the Middle East, for example—lend it a certain surface plausibility.

It is clearly time, then, for those who believe, as I do, that this recent explosion of aggressive millenarianism—what has come to be called Armageddon theology—is biblically and theologically perverse and historically dangerous, to say so plainly, and to give reasons for so saying. Such plain speaking may provide useful guidance for those troubled mainline Christians who don't quite know what to make of it all and for secularists, who may be tempted to dismiss it as merely bizarre and thus to miss the genuine historical and political threat that is resident within it.

MILLENARIAN EXPECTATIONS

What is it that this current crop of millenarians expects? Although prophets of the world's imminent end are not all agreed on the expected sequence of events, and some confusion arises from trying to collate their differences, the general expectation may be described as follows:

In the last days, the Soviet Union, along with other anti-Semitic nations allied with it (perhaps Germany, Iran, Ethiopia, and Turkey), will invade Israel. The Western alliance will offer only diplomatic protest. In desperation, Israel will turn to God, who will save it by supernatural intervention, probably a gigantic earthquake. The result will be confusion among the invading armies, who in their confusion will begin to do battle with one another. The earthquake will be accompanied by pestilence, flood, hail, and a rain of burning sulfur. The invading war machines will be unable to maneuver on the battlefield, and their troops will be decimated. All of this may occur on a single day.

Some believe that simultaneously with this destruction of the Communist military force, Communist agents throughout the world will be singled out by God for their own sudden destruction by means of a consuming fire. Says LaHaye, when that happens "we can only imagine the number of vacancies that will occur in one day in the federal and state governments and in the three thousand universities and colleges in America."

God's judgment against the Soviet Union, culminating in these acts of supernatural destruction, will occur, according to LaHaye, (1) because the Soviets are propagators of atheism, have "violated more biblical principles than any other nation," and have hated and persecuted the Jews; (2) to preserve Israel; and (3) "that then they [many nations] will know that I am the LORD" [Ezekiel 38; 23]. As a result of this stunning demonstration, millions around the world will now accept Christ as their Savior, though millions of others will persist in their unbelief.

With Communist military power utterly crushed and its worldwide network of subversion permanently destroyed, humanistic political leaders in the West will now move to create world government, a unification that will simply make it easier for that political figure known as the Anti-Christ to consolidate his power. He will be the leader of a ten-nation confederacy (the European Common Market?), will initially champion the cause of world peace, and will enter into a covenant with Israel guaranteeing its protection. At that moment, God will start a seven-year clock, a period known in "prophecy" as the Tribulation. For three-and-a-half years, the Anti-Christ will succeed in bringing peace and economic prosperity to the world and will survive an assassination attempt. Emboldened by his successes and accumulated power, and no longer needing to hide his true identity, he will gradually reveal his satanic intent. He will persecute Christians, who will be forbidden to work, buy, or sell. Many of them will be summarily executed. In an act described biblically as "the abomination of desolation standing where it ought not to stand," he will enter the Temple in Jerusalem and there declare himself to be God. The remaining three-and-a-half years will be a time of disaster and devastation unprecedented in all of human history. Teachers of "prophecy" believe that, 2,500 years ago, Ezekiel foretold those awful days that may occur within our own history:

. . . because of all your abominations I will do with you what I have never yet done, and the like of which I will never do again. Therefore fathers shall eat their sons in the midst of you, and sons shall eat their fathers; and I will execute judgments on you, and any of you who survive I will scatter to all the winds. Wherefore, as I live, says the Lord GOD, surely, because you have defiled my sanctuary with all your detestable things and with all your abominations, therefore I will cut you down; my eye will not spare, and I will have no pity. A third part of you shall die of pestilence and be consumed with famine in the midst of you; a third part shall fall by the sword round about you; and a third part I will scatter to all the winds and will unsheathe the sword after them. "Thus shall my anger spend itself, and I will vent my fury upon them and satisfy myself; and they shall know that I, the LORD, have spoken in my jealousy, when I spend my fury upon them."[1]

The Anti-Christ will make an alliance with a figure associated in "prophecy" with Babylon (sometimes understood as a symbol for Rome), one known as the False Prophet (sometimes identified by teachers of "prophecy" as the pope). An army from the East, perhaps made up of forces from China, India, and Japan, nations that worship false gods, will gather to mount an all-out attack on Jerusalem from a site overlooking the plain of Esdraelon, and the Battle of Armageddon will be on (in Hebrew, *Har-Megidon*, the hill of Megiddo, where many decisive battles in the history of ancient Israel were fought). The human carnage will be beyond imagination, and blood will flow "as high as a horse's bridle" for two hundred miles around Jerusalem (Revelation 14:20).

The destruction will not be confined to Jerusalem. By means that are unclear, whether human (nuclear missiles), natural (earthquakes), or supernatural, all of the great cities of the world will be obliterated.

At this point, Christ will return to earth in the sight of every human eye (by means of satellite television?), will intervene decisively in the battle, will cast the Anti-Christ and the False Prophet into hell, and will usher in a thousand-year golden age, the millennium. At the end of the thousand years, Satan will be released for a brief time so that the identity of those who, during the Tribulation and millennium, accepted Christ with their lips but not in their hearts can at last be revealed and brought to judgment. Says Hal Lindsey, "All who remain as mortals will be changed into immortality at this point, and the Kingdom of God [the millennium] will not cease, but simply change form and be reestablished in a new heaven and a new earth."

APOCALYPTIC VISIONS

What leads fundamentalist teachers of "prophecy" to expect these things? Many parts of the Bible are cast in a literary form known as "apocalyptic writing." The most prominent examples of this form are the Old Testament books of Ezekiel and Daniel and the New Testament book known as Revelation in English but whose Greek title is The Apocalypse of John. Less prominent examples are found in the thirteenth chapter of Mark and in the twenty-fourth and twenty-fifth chapters of Matthew. The chief characteristic of apocalyptic writing, especially in Ezekiel, Daniel, and Revelation, is the visions reported by their authors—visions that are full of angelic figures and fantastic beasts.

The author of Ezekiel reported a vision in which he encountered "the likenesses of four living creatures" in a great cloud:

> They had the form of men, but each had four faces, and each of them had four wings. Their legs were straight, and the soles of their feet were like the sole of a calf's foot; and they sparkled like burnished bronze. . . . And the four had their faces and their wings thus: their wings touched one another; they went every one straight forward, without turning as they went. As for the likeness of their faces, each had the face of a man in front; the four had the face of a lion on the right side, the four had the face of an ox on the left side, and the four had the face of an eagle at the back. Such were their faces.[2]

In a dream ascribed to Daniel, four beasts rise up out of the sea:

> The first was like a lion and had eagle's wings. Then as I looked its wings were plucked off, and it was lifted up from

the ground and made to stand upon two feet like a man; and the mind of a man was given to it. And behold, another beast, a second one, like a bear. It was raised up on one side; it had three ribs in its mouth between its teeth; and it was told, "Arise, devour much flesh." After this I looked, and lo, another, like a leopard, with four wings of a bird on its back; and the beast had four heads; and dominion was given to it. After this I saw in the night visions, and behold, a fourth beast, terrible and dreadful and exceeding strong; and it had great iron teeth; it devoured and broke in pieces, and stamped the residue with its feet. It was different from all the beasts that were before it; and it had ten horns. I considered the horns, and behold, there came up among them another horn, a little one, before which three of the first horns were plucked up by the roots; and behold, in this horn were eyes like the eyes of a man, and a mouth speaking great things.[3]

Strikingly similar are the visionary images of Revelation 13:

And I saw a beast rising out of the sea, with ten horns and seven heads, with ten diadems upon its horns and a blasphemous name upon its heads. And the beast that I saw was like a leopard, its feet were like a bear's, and its mouth was like a lion's mouth. And to it the dragon gave his power and his throne and great authority. One of its heads seemed to have a mortal wound, but its mortal wound was healed, and the whole earth followed the beast with wonder. . . . Then I saw another beast which rose out of the earth; it had two horns like a lamb and it spoke like a dragon. It exercises all the authority of the first beast in its presence, and makes the earth and its inhabitants worship the first beast, whose mortal wound was healed. . . . Also it causes all, both small and great, both rich and poor, both free and slave, to be marked on the right hand or the forehead, so that no one can buy or sell unless he has the mark, that is, the name of the beast or the number of its name. This calls for wisdom: let him who has understanding reckon the number of the beast, for it is a human number, its number is six hundred and sixty-six.[4]

The fundamentalist view of the Bible, examined in detail in chapter 3, holds that everything in the Bible is God's own direct and inerrant word. There is therefore nothing that is merely antiquarian in scripture, nothing without a saving significance. If everything in it is God's word, then everything must matter ultimately, if only we can be led to understand what that ultimate significance is. So, faced with Ezekiel and Daniel and Revelation, the fundamentalists are driven by their doctrine of the scriptures to find an interpretation that permits an urgent reading. And find it they do.

Fundamentalist interpreters of these so-called prophetic utterances believe that the beasts in the visions reported in the apocalyptic books refer explicitly and unmistakably to forces—persons, nations—not in some ancient history but in the present time. Therefore, the dreams and visions in those books contain a message that is intended for you and for me as for no other generations of Bible readers before us. Says one widely read book on "prophecy":

> One might ask, were not Biblical prophecies closed and sealed? Indeed they were—until now! And even *now* they can be understood *only* by those who possess the master key to unlock them!

> Daniel's prophecy . . . was not a message to . . . Israel . . . nor was it a message to Judah! . . . The plain truth is, these prophecies were written for OUR PEOPLE OF OUR TIME, and for no previous people or time! They pertain to world conditions TODAY, and could not have been understood *until* today! . . . It is emphatically clear that these prophecies pertain to NO TIME but to *our* time, in this Twentieth Century! [Emphases in the original][5]

If the dreams and visions of Ezekiel, Daniel, and Revelation refer to powers, persons, and events in our own time, then how should they be read? Not all fundamentalist interpreters of "prophecy" are agreed on those identifications, though that does not inhibit each individual interpreter from claiming that he possesses the *real* key by which God intends these portentous passages to be read.

Does the creature in Daniel, with the body of a lion and the wings of an eagle, represent the combined power of Great Britain and the United States? Those are, after all, the totemic figures with which the two nations are commonly identified. Is the bearlike creature the Soviet Union? Is the one like a leopard, with four wings and four heads, a group of powerful nations in Africa, which is the leopard's continent? Some would say so. On the one hand, the late Herbert W. Armstrong, founder of the Worldwide Church of God, believed that the United States and Britain are the lineal descendents of the lost tribes of Israel, with a great deal of biblical "prophecy" having to do with their special destiny in God's plan for the world. On the other hand, Hal Lindsey and Tim LaHaye insist that the United States is not explicitly referred to in "prophecy." Lindsey is sure, however, that Gog, king of Magog, in Ezekiel and the king of the North in Daniel both refer to the Soviet Union; he has identified the creature in Daniel with ten horns as the European Common Market.* The king of the South refers, he thinks, to a confederation of Arab states; and the king of the East is, predictably, China. And all of these visions are reputed to tell us exactly what the final conflict among these powers will be and where it will occur.

The number is, as Revelation 13 says, "the number of a man," and the quest for his identity has, over the centuries, been the world's most intriguing numbers game. We in the West long ago adopted the system of numeration used by the Arabs, and we sometimes use Roman numerals as well, especially to designate book chapters and years; but the ancient Hebrews and Greeks had no such independent numbering system. Instead they assigned numerical values to the letters of their alphabets. Since the New Testament was written in Greek to Christians who knew the Hebrew scriptures intimately, there were two levels on which 666 could be read: one as an ordinary number made up of three letters of the Greek alphabet, the other as the name of a man, the letters of whose name in Hebrew totaled 666. It is clear that the author of Revelation intended that his Christian readers should "reckon" the number to arrive at the second mean-

---

*But since this "prophecy" was made by Lindsey in 1970, the Common Market has grown to twelve nations, illustrating the danger of becoming too specific in one's "prophetic" identifications.

ing, one that would be inaccessible to the late-first-century Roman authorities who would see it merely as a number with no apparent significance.

It is contended that the long-hidden identity of the 666 man—that figure in our own late-twentieth-century history who is the real False Prophet foretold 1900 years ago by the seer of Revelation—can now be "reckoned" accurately by the elect, that is, by fundamentalist Christians. The rest of us, like the Romans, will be blind to the cipher's true meaning.

Unfortunately for the fundamentalist contention, teachers of "prophecy" have failed to agree on his identity. During World War II, some urged that Mussolini was Mr. 666, a conclusion drawn not from deriving numerical values from Hebrew or Greek but from assigning such values to the popular Italian salute "VIVA IL DUCE" and arriving at the required total. If numerical values are assigned to the English alphabet, such that H = 107, I = 108, T = 119, L = 111, E = 104, and R = 117, the result is HITLER. And if a different system is employed with English, so that A = 6, B = 12, C = 18, and so on, 666 turns out to be KISSINGER! Some time back Mary Stewart Relfe announced her "prudent assessment" that the False Prophet was Egypt's president Anwar Sadat. His subsequent "mortal wound"—he was downed by assassins—and the failure of that "mortal wound" to "heal" in conformity with Revelation 13, further illustrates the peril of precise identification. Most teachers of "prophecy," acutely aware of that peril and even more prudent than Relfe, exhibit a marked reluctance to name names. Herbert W. Armstrong was an exception, though by identifying an institution instead of an individual—he said the two beasts of Revelation 13, taken together, represent the Roman Catholic Church—he was less subject to direct refutation by subsequent events than was Relfe.

Dispensationalism, a feature of fundamentalism introduced in chapter 2, is another way of dealing with the issue of biblical inerrancy, and it has fired the millennial expectations of many, though not all, fundamentalists. One of the difficulties inherent in the inerrancy doctrine is the patent differences in outlook between the Old and New Testaments.

The law of Moses enjoined the Jews to do no murder; Jesus enjoined no anger. The law of Moses said no adultery; Jesus said no lust. The law of Moses required "an eye for an eye"; Jesus said, "Turn the other cheek."

How are these contrasts to be accommodated within a view that holds that everything in the Bible is to be received as God's command? John Nelson Darby, an Anglican priest who later became leader of the Plymouth Brethren around 1834, vigorously propagated the view that there are two scriptures, one for Jews and one for Christians, equally authoritative and intended by God for different people and involving different expectations. Darby, an avid millenarian, held that the "Tribulation," which would occur in the last days and whose coming would be marked by historical warning signs, would be experienced only by the Jews, whereas those faithful to Christ would experience a secret rapture, a gathering up to be with Christ, which would come utterly without warning. There is one "dispensation" for Jews, Darby taught, and another for Christians.

Cyrus Ingerson Scofield, the Congregational minister who became a convert to Darby's dispensational views around 1880, was primarily responsible for the widespread acceptance of dispensationalism among American fundamentalists. It has already been noted that the *Scofield Reference Bible*, with its elaborate system of interpretative notes accompanying the scriptural text, has been the most widely used study Bible since it first appeared in 1909. Among the most influential of those notes is the scheme of seven dispensational divisions in history, stretching from the creation to the millennium, in each of which God has set different expectations for humankind but with no evidence of progress in human obedience from one to the next. As each of the preceding five dispensations has ended in disaster, so the present dispensation, the sixth, will end in a "Tribulation" of enormous proportion, signaling the coming of the seventh and final age, the time of God's triumph over the satanic forces of disobedience in the universe.

Followers of dispensational millenarianism believed early in this century, and believe now, that organized Christianity is "falling into apostasy and heresy so deeply and so decisively that it [can] only mean the approach of the last days," as the historian Sydney Ahlstrom has described their view. Hence the spate of end-time teaching and writing described in earlier sections of this chapter. Today as in Darby's time, dispensationalism is espoused even by those who find no biblical evidence for a "secret rapture."

Finally among the influences that lead fundamentalists to their millenarian expectation is the claim made by teachers of "prophecy" that the visions of Ezekiel, Daniel, and Revelation are to be received as inerrant forecasts of present history because so much that those visions "predicted" has "come true" in our own time.

Chief among those fulfillments is the restoration of Israel to independent nationhood in 1948. Chapters 37 and 38 of Ezekiel are frequently cited by fundamentalists as the sources of this "prophecy," including the following passage in chapter 37:

> "Thus says the Lord GOD: Behold, I will open your graves, and raise you from your graves, O my people; and I will bring you home into the land of Israel. And you shall know that I am the LORD, when I open your graves, and raise you from your graves, O my people. And I will put my Spirit within you, and you shall live, and I will place you in your own land."[6]

According to Lindsey, the beast in Daniel 7 that had ten horns and the beast in Revelation 13 that had ten horns and ten diadems both contain an explicit anticipation of the federation known as the European Common Market. The "woman sitting on a scarlet beast, full of blasphemous names, having seven heads and 10 horns," envisioned in Revelation 17, prefigures the worldwide ecumenical movement of our time—i.e., the World Council of Churches—in Lindsey's view. He views that movement as an instrument of Satan because, while it professes faith in God, he sees it instead as a system of false worship, emasculating true faith in the interest of lowest-common-denominator theological compromise and substituting political pronouncement, on such matters as human rights and liberation movements, for sound doctrine. Hence, the blasphemy anticipated in the Revelation 17 passage.

In the view of Lindsey, LaHaye, and others, the rise of Russia into world superpower status, not even anticipated by its prominence in nineteenth-century European politics, was foreseen 2,500 years ago. The importance given in Ezekiel to Gog, king of Magog—Magog being the northern kingdom widely believed by purveyors of "prophecy" to refer to Russia, which kingdom will play a decisive role as Satan's instrument in the last days—makes sense to those purveyors only on the assumption that God revealed to Ezekiel, and to those in the present time who are permitted to read the signs faithfully, the exact shape of things to come. God's enmity against Russia, allegedly described in Ezekiel ("I am against you, O Gog, chief prince of Meshech and Tubal" [39:1]) anticipates official Soviet atheism, Soviet "hatred of the Jews," and the fact that the Soviet Union has become "the most evil government in the history of mankind," according to LaHaye. When, in history's last days, it commits a final outrage by moving arrogantly against Israel ("I will . . . bring you up from the uttermost parts of the north, and lead you against the mountains of Israel" [Ezekiel 39:2]), God will intervene and bring Russia to total annihilation as judgment upon all of its unspeakable and unparalleled sinfulness, so LaHaye teaches.

Nor is the Bible's purported prescience limited to historical events. Fundamentalists believe that its "prophecy" prefigures the technological developments of the present time. For example, we are told that the use of nuclear weapons in the last days is prefigured in Ezekiel 38:22 ("I will rain upon him . . . torrential rains and hailstones, fire and brimstone" [on Gog, king of Magog, and on his troops]) and in Zechariah 14:12 ("And this shall be the plague with which the LORD will smite all the peoples that wage war against Jerusalem: their flesh shall rot away while they are still on their feet, and their eyes shall rot in their sockets, and their tongues shall rot in their mouths"). It is also prefigured in 2 Peter 3:10 ("But the day of the Lord will come like a thief, and then the heavens will pass away with a loud noise, and the elements will be dissolved with fire, the earth and the works that are upon it will be burned up"). Satellite television is presumably prefigured in Revelation 1:7, where it is said that when Christ returns to earth, "every eye shall see him" simultaneously around the world.

A NONFUNDAMENTALIST CRITIQUE

What can be said in response to these things?

An Old Story Heard Before

The first thing that must be said is that we have heard it all before. We have heard the beasts of Daniel and Revelation identified in virtually every century with whatever powers and persons were in the ascendency at the moment. We have heard Revelation's malevolent 666 named, successively but hardly successfully, as Muhammed, Pope Benedict IX, Germany's Kaiser Wilhelm in World War I, Franklin Roosevelt, and the National Council of Churches, to name only an illustrious few in addition to those cited earlier in this chapter.

Basing their calculations on the same passages from Ezekiel, Daniel, 2 Peter, and Revelation, we have heard Joachim of Floris predict that the promised millennium would begin in 1260, and we have heard Christians who experienced the violent and frightening disruptions of the French Revolution announce that the end would come by 1800. We have heard William Miller's call to the faithful to prepare for Christ's second advent on October 22, 1843, have watched as the Millerites climbed to the rooftops, there to be caught up in the clouds with Christ, and have seen them climb down again the next morning. Earlier in this century, we have heard William Blackstone announce that the sure signs of that historical deterioration that heralds the immediate return of Christ were new modes of transportation, growing world literacy, and biblical criticism; pestilence, famine, and industrial conflict; and the rise of spiritualism, socialism, and Christian Science. We have heard Herbert W.

Armstrong's prediction that the end would come in January 1972, and we have seen members of his Worldwide Church of God preparing to leave for Petra in Jordan, which was thought to be a place of safety for the elect during the Tribulation.

And we have heard each of these pronounced with the same confident assurance that, however mistaken earlier millennial expectations may have been, this time we've got the scenario right! Given the repeated history of disillusionment, rooted in the misplaced confidence that God has given it to one generation to know the real meaning of the signs and symbols as no other generation before it has known them—this career of "prophetic" certainty followed by unvarying historical disappointment—we are entitled to conclude either (1) that God is a cruel trickster, or (2) that God had something else in mind in inspiring the writers of Ezekiel and Daniel and Revelation to apocalyptic utterance.

And there is one other thing we are hearing now that we have heard repeatedly in the past: a clear and, one would think for inerrantists, an embarrassing demonstration that those who assert the literal and plenary facticity of the Bible cannot agree on what its facts are. For example, in spite of the assertion that God has favored Christians living in this present moment of history with the key to decode the "prophetic" ciphers, the millennialists are unable to agree on how to read the message. Is the United States explicitly referred to in biblical "prophecy"? Herbert Armstrong and E.G. White say, decidedly yes! Lindsey and LaHaye say, decidedly no! Even more divisive within fundamentalism is the question of whether the "Rapture"—the raising up of true believers to be with Christ in the air, what Lindsey calls "the ultimate trip"—will occur *before* the great Tribulation, thereby rescuing the faithful from the terrors that will follow in that awful time, or *after* the Tribulation, in which case those terrors will plague and test believers as well as unbelievers. Lindsey and LaHaye, following the lead of the Scofield Bible, are pre-Tribulationists; David Terrell and Pat Robertson are post-Tribulationists. Further confounding the claim of God's authoritative disclosure, others—Mary Stewart Relfe is one—believe that the "Rapture" will occur mid-way into the Tribulation. Such disarray, which has been in evidence throughout the history of fundamentalism, scarcely comports with the claims for inerrancy that accompany it.

An Arrogant Misreading of Scripture and History

The second criticism to be made of Fundamentalist "prophecy" is that predictive fundamentalism of the kind described earlier in this chapter is an arrogant, self-centered, at the same time self-pitying and self-congratulatory, misreading both of scripture and of history. What it says, very plainly, is this: No one else who has ever read the Bible, throughout its hundreds of years, has read it accurately, properly, truthfully, until now. We [fundamentalists] know, as no one before us has known, what the truth is about the biblical witness. Augustine thought he knew, as did Luther and Calvin and Wesley; but God has finally given it to us to know that all of them were wrong and we are right!

In fact, it seems to me that if the predictive fundamentalists are right, then we must conclude that if Ezekiel and Daniel and the author of Revelation thought they understood the import of their own visions, they were wrong too. They appear to have assumed that they were saying something immediately meaningful, something of critical significance to their own contemporaries; but that can scarcely be true if their message was really intended for late-twentieth-century believers.

All this impresses me as simple arrogance, making a sham even of the fundamentalists' own biblical doctrine. Is the Bible the word of God? Fundamentalists tell us that it is. Has it always been so? If it is God's word, it cannot have been so at one time but not at another. It must always and everywhere have been the word of God. Was it the word of God, God's truth, for Augustine and Luther and Calvin and Wesley? Or was God merely playing with them, perhaps even deceiving them by not making the truth of his word plain to them, having intended to wait until the present time to make the truth plain to us as to no generation before us? Such a view mocks the notion of a trustworthy God.

Predictive fundamentalism is at once self-pitying and self-congratulatory. It is self-pitying because it says our time is worse than any other time in human history, our problems greater, the evil in our world more magnified. Nobody else in recorded time has suffered as we are suffering, and that is the way we know that the end time is near. Our unprecedented extremity is its sure sign. So the pity runs. And with it the self-congratulation: Just because of our extremity, God has chosen to let us in on the real truth of things.

Of course we live in tough times. But is our late twentieth century really darker than, say, the fourteenth, that hapless era so impressively chronicled by Barbara Tuchman in *A Distant Mirror?* That was the century when, during two terrible years, the Black Death killed more than a third of the population from Iceland to India, returning four more times before the era was up. It was the century when gangs of terrorists plundered Europe without hindrance; when the Hundred Years' War took on a life of its own, frustrating efforts to end it, unfolding in "an epic of brutality and bravery checkered by disgrace." It was a time when new weapons and errant knighthood brought an end to chivalry, when widespread peasant revolt was answered by terrible autocratic repression, and when internal scandal robbed the church of its ability to comfort and to save.

Is the present time worse than that? I doubt it very much, and it is self-pitying arrogance to believe that it is. History does not give us reliable means for measuring its darkest days; and in any event, I see no evidence that the problems of the present are in greater disproportion to the resources available for their solution than in earlier periods of human experience.

A Perverted View of Biblical Prophecy

A third criticism is that the millenarian view—that Ezekiel and Daniel and Revelation are "prophecies" for our own time as for no other time before our own—is rooted in a fundamentalist perversion of what it means, biblically, to be a prophet. The Hebrew word *nabi* and the Greek word *prophētēs*, both of which are translated as "prophet" in the Old and New Testaments, have virtually the same meaning: speaker, spokesperson, one who bears witness. The prophet—whether he be Isaiah or Amos, or one of the obscure writers of Ezekiel and Daniel and Revelation—is a testifier to the will and the judgment of God within the concrete historical events of his own times. It is not merely incidental, for instance, that Isaiah located his stunning vision, recounted in chapter 6 of his prophecy, "in the year that king Uzziah died." That phrase provided its indispensable setting, tying the vision and its message explicitly to the national crisis created by the death of a ruler whose long and esteemed reign had brought prosperity and stability to the nation. The prophets of the Old and New Testaments are the moral interpreters of the events through which God's people are passing. Sometimes they are testifiers to the waywardness of the people and proclaimers of the righteousness to which God calls individuals and nations. They say to their contemporaries, "Our God is a demanding God, and if you continue in your evil ways, worshiping false gods, oppressing the poor and the captive, defying the moral law, God will bring you down, even if he has to use the power of a pagan Persia or Assyria to do it." Sometimes the prophets witness to the compassion of God for the suffering through which God's people are passing at the hands of others— Egypt, Babylon—offering God's strength for endurance and the hope that in due course God will confound the tyrant and restore his people to strength and health.

That is the nature of biblical prophecy: the exposure of sin, whether of Israel or of its enemies, and the declaration of the consequences of sin in a world in which God is the ultimate sovereign: judgment for sinners and compassion for the suffering. God sent prophets to a peculiar people, in the midst of a peculiar situation, to announce a peculiar judgment and to offer a peculiar redemption. Isaiah was calling Israelites of the eighth century B.C. to account; he was not talking over their heads to us today. The writer of Daniel was calling

Israel's Syrian oppressor to account in the second century
B.C. and urging the Jews to remain faithful because God
would bring that evil oppressor down; he was not talking
over their heads to us. John of Revelation was calling the
Roman authorities about A.D. 96 to account for their brutal
persecution of Christians and urging the persecuted to remain faithful because God would bring the evil persecutor
down; he was not talking over their heads to the twentieth
century. Thus there is no need, by ingenious and sometimes
disingenuous speculation, to seek a late-twentieth-century
identity for the 666 man. The seer's own time provided a
fully adequate Hebrew translation for that cipher: *Neron
Caesar* (or Nero Caesar, which accounts for the variant reading 616 that appears in some ancient manuscripts). It was
widely believed, in the late-first-century Roman world, that
the emperor Nero would come back to life, a prospect for
Christians that would have been even more crushing than
the brutalisms they were already suffering under the emperor Domitian at the time Revelation was written. Nero had
come to be the symbolic epitome of everything satanic;
hence his appearance as 666, the bestial regent of Satan in
Revelation 13.

Thus the biblical prophet is not primarily a predictor of
coming events but a witness to the moral character and
consequences of events in his own time. To be sure, some of
those consequences will occur in the future: in spite of the
appearance of unrelieved disaster represented in Israel's
Babylonian Captivity, God intends to restore Israel to its
Palestinian patrimony and its sovereign nationhood. But for
the prophet, it is the relatively short-term future of those
who are in the midst of the prophecies, not a future—our
own twentieth century, for example—that neither he nor
they could possibly envision or comprehend.

Sometimes there is, in the prophets, a specific prediction:
Hananiah is identified as a "false prophet." Therefore,
Jeremiah declares, "thus says the LORD: '. . . This very year
you shall die,'" and further records that, in fact, Hananiah
did die in the seventh month of that year (28:16–17). But that
is by no means the primary mode of prophetic utterance, as

has already been seen. Sometimes what appears to be the foretelling of events is, in fact, ex *post facto* "prophecy," written *after* the events as an interpretation of them. It was common, in Jewish apocalyptic writing, to identify authorship with some admirable figure in Jewish history. So the book of Daniel purports to have been written during the sixth century B.C., when the Jews were suffering under the fierce yoke of Babylon, by one Daniel, a Jewish hero named in Ezekiel. In fact, literary evidence supports the view that Daniel was written by an anonymous author some time after 168 B.C., when the Jews were suffering under the no-less-fierce yoke of Antiochus Epiphanes IV of Syria, whose sacrilegious installation of an altar to Zeus in the Jerusalem Temple was the "abomination of desolation" of Daniel 11:31. Thus the so-called prophecies contained in Daniel provided an interpretation of events that had already come to pass before they were written.

The relevance of Ezekiel and Daniel and Revelation to the present historical situation is precisely what it was for those to whom those writings were first addressed. God is still sovereign. Sin and evil still have consequences. God still comforts those who suffer and is actively at work to turn tough times to redemptive purpose. Having seen God's judgment in an earlier period prepares us today to identify that which deserves judgment in our own history. Having heard God's prophets encourage faithfulness even under the most severe provocations in the past, we are strengthened in our own faithfulness in trying times.

There is one other consideration, more theological than biblical, and it has to do with the fundamentalist notion that God has given to the recorders of scripture—to Ezekiel and to John of Revelation—an inerrant account of history before it happens; that God has told them infallibly, in the sixth century B.C. or in the closing years of the first century A.D., about events that will occur toward the end of the twentieth century A.D. What is foreknown is predetermined; there can be no unmistakable knowledge of events without the power of absolute external control over those events. Where there is absolute external control, there can be no responsibility assigned to actors within those events. Where there is no individual responsibility, there is no sin. Where there is no sin, there can be no judgment. And if there were no judgment, Tribulation and Armageddon would be the egregious and wanton acts of a terrorist deity. It's as simple as that!

A Highly Selective Use of Scripture

Fourth, current claims for the imminent end of history depend for their authorization on a highly selective use of scripture. It must be admitted at once that there is, indeed, a strong apocalyptic strain in the Gospels, with anticipation of the Parousia—the return of Christ—in Acts, in the epistles, and in Revelation. Late in the last century and earlier in this one, liberal scholars tried to read Jesus' teaching about the coming kingdom of God with evolutionary import, seizing upon the mustard-seed parable, for example, as evidence that Jesus expected the kingdom to grow and unfold gradually over time. But Albert Schweitzer's *The Quest of the Historical Jesus*, first published in English in 1910, shattered that liberal distortion and thereafter made it impossible to ignore the apocalyptic element that is present in his teaching.

Two things must be said about New Testament apocalypticism, however, both of which are ignored, or quite unacceptably interpreted away, by the teachers of "prophecy." One is that *the end was clearly expected to occur within the apostolic generation to which Jesus spoke.* For example, in Matthew 16:28 Jesus says: "Truly, I say to you, there are some standing here who will not taste death before they see the Son of man coming in his kingdom." And in Matthew 24:34: "Truly, I say to you, this generation will not pass away till all these things take place." And when Jesus advised his hearers, in Luke 17:31, on their proper behavior when the end should break in ("On that day, let him who is on the housetop, with his goods in the house, not come down to take them away; and likewise let him who is in the field not turn back"), both he and they appeared to understand that the advice was intended specifically for them.

Paul carried that sense of immediacy with him especially in his early ministry. He told the Thessalonian Christians that "we who are alive, who are left, shall be caught up together with them [who have already died in the faith] in the clouds to meet the Lord in the air" (1 Thessalonians 4:17). And to the Corinthians he said reassuringly that "we shall not all sleep [that is, die]" before Christ comes again (1 Corinthians 15:51).

So for much, perhaps most, of the New Testament, the expectation of God's in-breaking was a *present* historical expectation for its own time, not a projection into a future 1900 years distant.

In the later writings of the New Testament, there is evidence of a growing concern at the delay of the Parousia. The Epistle of James, written near the end of the first century A.D., counsels, "Be patient . . . until the coming of the Lord," urging a forbearance like that of Job (5:7–11). Second Peter, which was written even later, probably some time after A.D. 100, acknowledges the presence of "scoffers" who say, "Where is the promise of [Christ's] coming?" Its author (who is not the apostle Peter but a much later and otherwise unknown Christian who believed that his writing was consonant with apostolic teaching) acknowledges that the apostolic generation is gone and "all things have continued as they were from the beginning of creation," which is to say that the radical change in history anticipated in the expectation of an early return of Christ simply has not happened. But, says the epistle's author, God's time is not our time, since "with the Lord one day is a thousand years." What is imminent in God's time may not be imminent as we count time. Furthermore, what may appear to be slowness on God's part is, in fact, an act of mercy, providing time for repentance, since God desires that none should perish in a final judgment (2 Peter 3:3–9).

Some of the later writings appear to spiritualize and make inward what was originally expected to be a public event. Paul himself may have prepared the way for that spiritualizing. In Colossians, probably written ten years after 2 Thessalonians, with its expectation of the Parousia still vivid, Paul wrote that Christ "has delivered us from the dominion of darkness and transferred us to the kingdom of his beloved Son, in whom we have redemption, the forgiveness of sins" (Colossians 1:13–14). What was to come as a historical occurrence, in 2 Thessalonians, has become a present spiritual reality, in Colossians. The Fourth Gospel, written thirty years or more after the last of Paul's letters, may intend to substitute the promise of a "comforter" or "counselor" (usually understood as the Holy Spirit) "to be with you forever" as a guide to the way, truth, and life announced in Jesus' earthly ministry. That promise would be difficult to interpret if there had been a lively expectation of the imminent return of Christ himself at the time the Gospel was written. And the epistle of 1 John, written about the same time as the Gospel, reflects a similar view that what was expected historically is already happening spiritually: "I am writing you a new commandment, which is true in him [God] and in you, because the darkness is passing away and the true light is already shining" [1 John 2:8].

In spite of the lengthening delay of the Parousia within the New Testament period, the church that formed the New Testament did not excise the more immediate expectation from the earlier parts of the canon. It is still there to trouble and confound us.

The second thing to be said about New Testament apocalyptic teaching has to do with the *unpredictable* nature of God's action to end history. In Acts, where Luke records Jesus' last words before the ascension, a disciple asks, "Lord, will you at this time restore the kingdom to Israel?" And Jesus replies, bluntly and unequivocally, "It is not for you to know times or seasons which the Father has fixed by his own authority" [1:6–7]. It was by no means the first time he had spoken that way. When Pharisees asked when the kingdom was coming, he told them, "The kingdom of God is not coming with signs to be observed; nor will they say, 'Lo, here it is!' or 'There!' for behold, the kingdom of God is in the midst of you." And if anyone does say, "Lo, there!" or "Lo, here!" they are not to be followed (Luke 17:20–23). Similarly, when disciples ask for "the signs that these things are all to be accomplished," Jesus warns them against false prophets and against unreliable signs: "when you hear of wars and rumors of wars, do not be alarmed; . . . the end is not yet" [Mark 13:4–7, 21–23].

Paul offered a similar warning to the Thessalonians: "But as to the times and the seasons, brethren, you have no need to have anything written to you. For you yourselves know well that the day of the Lord will come like a thief in the night" [1 Thessalonians 5:1–2], a simile that reappears in 2 Peter 3:10.

Indeed, whenever in the Gospels the question of the in-breaking of God's kingdom comes up, Jesus' emphasis is not on prediction, not on "prophesying," but on *readiness*. He says, in effect, "Don't wait until you think you see the signs of its coming, for those signs will probably be false anyway. God will choose his own time. Rather, *be ready at every moment by living, in every moment, a life which is commendable to God*. Then whenever he calls, in the sudden unexpectedness of his own will and way, you will be ready."

When they fail to give these two characteristics of New Testament apocalyptic—its sense of immediacy and its imperative to readiness—their full, literal due, teachers of biblical "prophecy" distort the scriptural witness to serve their own historical and dogmatic predilections.

An Excuse for Reprehensible Behavior

A fifth criticism is that rather than creating a greater faithfulness—readiness—as Jesus apparently intended, the "Armageddon theology" of our own time provides for some men and women an excuse for engaging in forms of personal, social, and political behavior that are, by any proper Christian standard, reprehensible.

Listen to what some teachers of "prophecy" are saying, and see how often their message is either subtly or flagrantly anti-Jewish, anti-Arab, anti-Catholic, antihomosexual, anti-abortionist, and antihumanist. By dehumanizing—indeed, by bestializing—the Soviets, fundamentalists give themselves a good conscience about their special hatred of the

Soviet Union and the annihilation they believe God has in store for that nation in the last days. LaHaye teaches that while God is *"for* mankind," he is against the Soviet Union, which must mean that in the divine reckoning (or at least in LaHaye's) the Soviet Union is not a part of "mankind." Whereas ordinary human beings can sin and be forgiven through belief in Christ, "the satanic presence that indwells the Russian leaders" places them beyond forgiveness and marks them for divine destruction, in LaHaye's view.* The "prophetic" movement is, in many of its forms, a movement of againstness, and the LaHaye reasoning could be used to exclude any of those it opposes from the ordinary considerations of a Christian compassion. The language used by the movement in describing the Tribulation is a language of terrible violence, and it appears to take pleasure from the prospect that God's "enemies" will suffer unspeakably when it comes—feeling free, of course, to make assumptions about who God's enemies are that God may not be making!

In an article titled "Waiting for the End," sociologist William Martin reported that followers of "prophecy" have borrowed money with no intention whatever of paying it back, believing that the end will come before the note falls due.

At the level of national policy, it is permissible for fundamentalists to permit the despoliation of the American wilderness because, with the end near, we are no longer required to worry about the consequences of that despoliation for future generations. When Interior Secretary-designate James Watt said, at his Senate confirmation hearing, "I do not know how many future generations we can count on before the Lord returns," his subsequent disclaimer that he did not mean that the Interior Department under his direction would not be concerned with the long-term management of our natural treasures, was hardly persuasive.

---

*It is, at the very least, a tragic coincidence that the convicted Nazi war criminal Alois Brunner, chief aide to Adolf Eichmann, justified the extermination of the Jews with similar "logic." "All of them deserved to die," said Brunner, "because *they were the devil's agents* and human garbage" (emphasis added).

At the level of foreign policy, journalist Grace Halsell reports, in her book *Prophecy and Politics: Militant Evangelists on the Road to Nuclear War,* that there is an alarming alliance between fundamentalism and the most militant factions of Zionism. As has already been seen, fundamentalists believe that the reestablishment of Israel as a nation is the "prophetic" precondition for the return of Christ. They have therefore been among the most zealous supporters of the pro-Israeli policies of a succession of United States presidents, have opposed the claims of the surrounding Arab states because those states threaten the continued existence of Israel as a national entity, and have ignored the plight of the Palestinian refugees, including a large body of Christian Arabs, who are the hapless victims of the Israeli-Arab enmity. It is, in fact, an odd and morally anomalous alliance. The Israelis have welcomed the open support of fundamentalist leaders such as Falwell and Swaggart, because those evangelists can mobilize enormous pressure on American administrations to provide virtually uncritical economic and military support for Israel. Yet, for their part, fundamentalists believe that once the establishment of Israel permits God's clock to tick toward the Tribulation and the final battle on the Plain of Megiddo, the Jews will be delivered only if they acknowledge at last that Jesus is the true messiah. Jews who remain faithful to their own traditions will be destroyed like any other unbeliever. Says Halsell, the fundamentalist "loves Israel but does not especially like the Jews. He seems to have little or no remorse for Jews and others he says will be killed" in the end times, nor does he experience any moral distress in the fact that his present "befriending" of Israel has as its ultimate purpose the final destruction of Judaism!

Halsell also reports that under the pressure of "prophetic" expectation, some fundamentalists are providing active financial and political support for Israeli terrorists who plot to destroy the sacred Muslim Dome of the Rock and its Al-Aqsa mosque in Jerusalem, even though the resultant rage throughout the Arab world might ignite World War III. Jewish zealots believe that the historic Second Temple of Judaism, destroyed in A.D. 70, once stood there and that a new Third Temple must be built to redeem the place from its present Muslin desecration and to restore the ancient Hebrew practice of animal sacrifice. Fundamentalists have their own reason for providing direct support for the terrorists: they believe Ezekiel 44 "prophesies" that in the last days the Jews will have reinstated animal sacrifice in a rebuilt Temple and that in assisting with the fulfillment of that "prophecy" they can hasten the arrival of those end times.

At the level of military policy, it is possible to fire up the arms race, and to create nuclear confrontation with the Soviet Union, because all of that may make things worse and thereby speed the end. Said evangelist Pat Robertson, "We are not to weep as the people of the world weep when there are certain tragedies or break-ups of the government or the systems of the world. We are not to wring our hands and say, 'Isn't that awful?' That isn't awful at all. It's good. That is a token, an evident token of our salvation, of where God is going to take us."

So if we do not choose to help make things worse, we can at least have a good conscience about resigning from responsible participation in the world. So much for seeking to alleviate world hunger or to ease the plight of refugees; so much for mitigating the reach of the terrorist and the torturer; so much for trying to reduce violence or disorder or family breakup. For only as these things worsen will God finally intervene decisively.

Strange behavior from those who profess to believe a Bible that tells us that anyone who says, "I love God" and hates his brother is a liar; that tells us that "God was in Christ, reconciling the world to himself, not counting their trespasses against them, and committing to us the ministry of reconciliation." Strange behavior from those who profess to love a Lord whose mission was to the poor, the blind, the bruised, the captive, and who called his followers to be peacemakers.

In *Born Againism*, Eric Gritsch strikes what impresses me as a more authentic Christian note:

Christ calls believers into service in this world, not into a position of waiting for the world to come. Christian teaching about the end time . . . does not call us to speculate about the end time, but to be alert to the "signs of the times" which provide clues to what needs to be done now in this world. . . .

The gospel calls for a cruciform life on earth, that is, a life fully aware of sin, evil, and death, yet committed to the living Lord who will come at the end of time. To be oriented exclusively toward the end time can be the signal that Christian hope has been paralyzed by the fear that faith is without influence in the world.[7]

In other words—and this is my conclusion rather than Gritsch's—the Armageddon theology of our time is a form of unbelief!

Traducing the Character of God in Christ

Finally, when the followers of "prophecy" teach that God will visit the earth with a time of tribulation beyond any previous suffering humankind has experienced, they traduce the character of the God whom we come to know in Jesus as the Christ.

Recall the way Ezekiel described a time of unprecedented tribulation, as the followers of "prophecy" expect it to occur in the last days:

And because of all your abominations I will do with you what I have never yet done, and the like of which I will never do again. . . . I will cut you down; my eye will not spare, and I will have no pity. A third part of you shall die of pestilence and be consumed with famine in the midst of you; a third part shall fall by the sword round about you; and a third part I will scatter to all the winds and will unsheathe the sword after them.[8]

Is that the God of whom Jesus taught, the God that makes the rain to fall upon the just and the unjust, the God that causes the sun to shine on the evil and on the good? The shepherd who leaves the ninety and nine and goes in search of one who has strayed? The father who neglects the son who has stayed at home in order to watch for the return of the prodigal one who deliberately walked away from his father's house? The God who loves not only sinners but this imperfect world, sending his own Son, as the Fourth Gospel tells us, not to condemn the world, but that the world through him might be saved?

Would you deliberately infect your neighbors with deadly pestilence? Would you starve them deliberately? Would you kill them wantonly? Surely not! Then is your goodness, or mine—is our compassion, our proactive love—greater than God's? Surely not! Jesus taught that we should love our enemies and forgive those who persecute us unjustly. Would God do less? Is our forbearance and capacity for forgiveness to be greater than God's? Surely not. We are to be "perfect" in direct imitation of God's perfection. Jesus said, "If you being evil know how to give good things to your children, how much more shall God give good things to those that ask him." The difference between ourselves and God, Jesus tells us, is that God is not less loving but more loving, not less forgiving but more forgiving, not less persistent in seeking the good of all including his enemies but more persistent, not less willing to give good things to the undeserving but more willing.

I, for one, cannot believe in the God whom Jesus reveals and at the same time believe that God would deliberately visit upon the world a tribulation worse than all of the death camps of Germany and the Soviet Union, and all of the unremitting torture of Latin American regimes, and all of the diseases and natural disasters that have ever occurred, and all of the nuclear arsenals set off at once—all at one time. Surely that makes a mockery of saying that God is love!

In biblical times, the Jews expected a messiah who would come with flaming sword, conquering and to conquer, calling down the hosts of heaven to destroy all who did not bear the mark of God's elect, thereby purifying and clearing the earth for God's kingdom. Jesus faced the temptation to be that kind of messiah, but he believed the temptation came from the Devil, and he turned his back deliberately and decisively upon it. Because of that refusal, he was confidently misunderstood by his Jewish-Christian disciples and rejected by the public at large, once the events beyond Palm Sunday began to unfold. Jesus taught, instead, that he had come, not to destroy sinners but to seek and to save that which was lost, not to cause suffering but to heal the sufferers, not to establish an earthly kingdom but to confirm a spiritual one, not to perpetrate a violent triumph by taking the lives of others but to win through his own suffering and death and by that unearthly means to set loose the power of salvation in the world.

When asked some years ago by a college student, "Is there a hell?" Gordon Poteat said after a thoughtful silence, "If there is a hell, Jesus is in it." He meant, by that striking and enigmatic sentence, to say that the New Testament leads us to expect Jesus always to be actively at work in the place of greatest human need.

Satan would host a holocaust. Jesus would not!

A CHRISTIAN STANCE

If anyone should wonder why this movement of biblical "prophecy" has reached such dimension now, the answer is surely clear: Everything seems to be out of control. The family is coming apart, traditional values are being overturned, the economy is in a virtual shambles, technology advances so fast that we can't keep up, conflict among nations seems impossibly complex and irreversible. So there is frustration, disappointment, fear, resignation, and anger, all in vast proportion.

And there is also, in view of the outsized nature of these problems, an enormous loss of nerve, a despair at the possibility of ordinary men and women bringing any kind of good out of this incredible mess. So it seems that only the radical intervention of God can save us.

Well, that point of view simply won't do! It is, in fact, evidence of unbelief. To be a Christian surely means living in the confidence that God has *already* intervened decisively in history, setting loose in the life and death and resurrection of Jesus as the Christ all of the transforming power the world needs. To be a Christian means to conform one's life actively and responsibly to that power and to let it do its transforming work in and through that life.

Perhaps the end of the world *is* near. I do not know what incredibly foolish things individuals and nations will permit themselves to fall into in the near future, what compacts we will make with hell through the projected use of nuclear and biological weapons, what ecological disasters we will actively perpetrate or merely permit to happen, and withal what unprecedented human tragedy we will willingly or witlessly sponsor. I only know that if there is danger of the imminent destruction of the world, God's hand is not in it. And if I am to be God's man for this moment, it will be my obligation to work with God to see that it doesn't happen!

CHAPTER 6

What We Can Learn from the Fundamentalists

HOWEVER MUCH WE MAY DISAGREE with a particular point of view, there is always, in the economy of things, something positive it can teach us. In the case of fundamentalism, its theological and behavioral excesses should not prevent us from acknowledging the points at which it has put its collective finger on some things that are genuinely and permanently important. The purpose of this final chapter is to identify eight propositions on which nonfundamentalists may be able to join with fundamentalists in common affirmation.

NEWER, NOT BETTER

Newer is not necessarily better. In fact, newer is not necessarily newer; that is, the past is sometimes more advanced than the present. It was one of the errors of an earlier liberalism that it assumed history to be on an upward escalator. The concept of evolution, which was the single most influential idea in the late nineteenth and early twentieth centuries, came to be applied not only to the physical development of organisms but to human spiritual and moral development as well. In character as in physiology, in intellect as in genes, history was seen to be moving steadily from the cruder to the more refined, from the more primitive to the more sophisticated.

So liberal scholars came to believe that if the several distinct literary units within the Bible—both entire books and parts of books—were placed, not in the order in which they have been arranged traditionally, not in the order in which the books themselves purport to have been written (the text of Daniel, for example, represents itself as coming out of the seventh century B.C.), but in the order in which liberal scholars believed those units were actually written (Daniel, they concluded, was in fact the product of the second century B.C.), then one would find an evolution of biblical ideas from the oldest to the latest. For example, they believed that chronological arrangement showed the concept of God moving from that of a crude tribal deity whose influence was limited to a relatively small geographical area, in the earliest writings, to a universal Spirit whose power and influence pervaded the whole of the universe, in the latest writings. Morality, they thought, would be seen to move progressively from primitive tribal instincts tied to narrow self-interest, in the earliest, to an ethic of universal love extending even to the enemy, in the latest.

More recent biblical scholarship has shown that liberal evolutionary interpretation to be a fiction. Rather than supporting a simple and simple-minded unidirectional scheme, the biblical record shows something far more complex: it shows the crude and the elevated often existing side by side in the same period throughout its narrative stretching over twelve centuries or more. If the calculating "eye for an eye" morality of Deuteronomy came, in its present form, from a seventh-century editor, as much scholarship now believes, the quite uncalculating love ethic of the prophet Hosea appeared a hundred years earlier. So much for moral evolution!

In the twentieth century, Gandhi and Hitler coexisted. In character, Francis of Assissi was light years ahead of the grasping and greedy traders of Wall Street. Shakespeare in literature, Bach and Mozart in music, set standards for creativity to which twentieth-century art must submit itself for judgment.

To understand that newer is not necessarily better does not require us to absolutize the past and to oppose change, as fundamentalists have done, but rather to honor the past and to be discriminating about change. It means refusing to embrace every change as if, by virtue of its newness, it must be greeted as progress. It means rejecting the notion that history gives us permission to do whatever it puts newly within our power to do. Jacques Ellul seems to be right: "Everything that is technique is necessarily used as soon as it is available, without distinction of good or evil. This is the principal law of our age." Those who intend to be discriminating about change will seek the repeal of that law. D.T. Niles was right when he said that one of the most urgent tasks of Christians is "the discovery of what brilliantly successful methods must now be discarded because they are not faithful to the gospel of Jesus Christ."

At the same time, to understand that newer is not necessarily better means that, while we reverence an ancient scripture and acknowledge its present claim upon us, we may also believe, as fundamentalists seem not to do, that God is in our future, and that "there is yet more light to break forth" from that ancient Word.

THE LIMITATIONS OF SCIENCE

Science, like every other human enterprise, is limited in its significance and competence. If we must resist fundamentalism's efforts to set the Bible over against modern inquiry, and its insistence that Genesis gives us a credible science to be preferred over contemporary paleontology and cosmology, we can nevertheless be grateful for the fundamentalist recognition that science is an incomplete enterprise, and for its unwillingness to cede to science an authority in matters that touch on meanings and morals, for which science has no competence.

While fundamentalism has sought to subordinate science to religion, some people in this modern era have believed, on the contrary, that religion ought to be subordinated to science, or even more boldly that science has now made religion obsolete and therefore entirely dispensable. Given the extent to which science has penetrated the unknown and freed modern men and women from a disabling ignorance, it should now be possible for the intellectually liberated to accept scientific explanations of the world without recourse to the metaphors and mythologies religion has traditionally supplied. Religion is speculative and raises questions; science is factual and certain. Increasingly as science is able to demonstrate the way the world really is, mature men and women should no longer have need for religious refuge. So a popular argument goes in these modern times.

Nowhere in history has there been such a deliberate and systematic attempt to root out and tear up all vestiges of religion as in the Soviet Union. There the authorities have given legal and repressive force to the proposition that humankind "come of age," meaning, that is, the "new" humankind shaped by scientific socialism, has no need of religion in any form. Yet the ideology and institution of Soviet Communism would collapse were it not for the religious apparatus its creators have constructed to replace the traditional one they have suppressed. Official Soviet life has its holy days and its rituals, its sacramental rites of passage, its creeds and inspired writings, and its saints whose relics, interred in the Kremlin wall, are the objects of a popular veneration. Like the Vatican, the Kremlin occasionally revises its authorized hagiography as former saints become nonpersons. And all of this is done without the faintest glimmer of recognition that supposedly scientific socialism is, in fact, grounded in myth and cultus.

Religion is, indeed, reformable, as in the Soviet Union; moreover, it regularly requires reformation for its own reinvigoration and relevance. But religion is not eradicable; it is not replaceable by science for the reason that science treats only of ignorance, while religion treats of mystery. The two, ignorance and mystery, are not the same in spite of a popular usage that makes them synonymous. Ignorance has to do with the temporarily unknown; mystery has to do with the eternally hidden. Both are in us and around us. When I do not know how to cure the virus that saps my energy, that is ignorance; but when I do not know how to make sense out of my inexorable journey toward death, that is mystery. When I do not know the distance to the farthest galaxy, that is ignorance; but when I do not know why this world exists and not some other, that is mystery.

It is the function of science to discover evidence for proximate solutions; it is the function of religion to discern meaning in the ultimates that cannot be solved. A world in which science was omnicompetent and religion obsolete would be a world without mystery; but that would be an altogether different world from the one in which, without our consent and against all of our contrary efforts, we are placed.

The great creative scientists know this. Those speculative inquirers who are at work out on the leading edges of scientific knowledge daily meet realities that cannot be quantified, that defy efforts to crowd them back into the comfortable systems that lesser intellects have built to contain the universe, that can be talked about only in a language that is closer to myth than to math. Those great scientists regularly experience reality as it was once expressed by the late Bishop Gerald Kennedy:

> The physical universe is not all that we once thought it was. The so-called solid stuff is not solid. What we once thought was stationary mass is really whirling energy. Electrons may be particles or they may be waves, and the physicist has to use an equation that will work in either case. You might call it chance, or you might suggest that the universe has a kind of free will. Apparently our picture of the world as a machine is no longer a fitting one. The universe is more like an idea, and it seems to have less and less the likeness of a closed system. Even here, then, the wildness lies in wait.[1]

The great creative scientists, out on the leading edges of knowledge, know this. It is only the rest of us, lesser scientists and ill-informed lay persons, far removed from the frontiers and preoccupied with smaller and more measurable matters, who are still tempted to think that nothing eventually can defy our organized cleverness. We still try to live by that "cosmic impiety" that even the atheist philosopher and scientist Bertrand Russell saw as "the greatest danger of our time" because of the "vast social disaster" to which such human pride and presumption must inevitably lead.

Max Otto, proud atheist though he was in religion and scientific humanist in philosophy, could nevertheless insist that, "whether we admit it or not there is always an unexplored beyond, always mystery."

> A conscious awareness of this mystery does healing work on the inward man. It is the healing work of acknowledged ignorance in the revered presence of that which eludes comprehension—the incomprehensible in each other, in the life we are called upon to live, in the great cosmic setting that reaches from our feet to the infinities.[2]

THE CENTRALITY OF THE BIBLE

The Bible is the source and center of the Christian faith. If we must reject the fundamentalists' insistence on an inerrant scripture because that often sets the Bible against itself and sometimes gives us a petulant, parochial, capricious God, we can nevertheless be grateful for the fundamentalists' witness to the centrality of the scriptures for the Christian faith and for their demand that the Bible be read with ultimate seriousness.

Fundamentalism, as has been shown, insists that the Bible has the Holy Spirit for its author, under whose direction men wrote as they were inspired to write. Some earlier liberals, fascinated and sometimes fixated by the human influences on biblical composition and transmission that their scholarship was then revealing, said that the Bible is, rather, an astonishing record of human achievement, an account of the increasingly clearer perception biblical men and women had of the character and intent of God, the story of an unparalleled struggle upward toward transcendent truth and moral elevation.

Each was partly right. Fundamentalists have been right in insisting that the central significance of the Bible is that it records not a human search but a divine initiative; not a persistent effort to bridge the gap between the finite and the infinite from the human side, which ends as often as not in some kind of idolatry, but the account of God's own persistence in reaching out to men and women in spite of their frequent spiritual obtuseness and arrogance. Liberals have been right in insisting that the Bible is a very human document, in the sense that it came not out of some passionless mechanical process but out of the passionate conviction of its writers that something ultimate had happened to them and to their fellows, not out of the compulsion of divine dictation but out of the compulsion of their own astonishment and gratitude. It is a very human document in the sense that it is a record in which we can find ourselves; in which women and men not unlike us—often spiritually obtuse and arrogant—recount events at once intimate and ultimate in which, remarkably, they believed they had been grasped by God beyond any power of their own grasping, confronted by God as surely and as unmistakably as they confronted one another; in which they were judged by God, known more surely than they knew one another, or even than they knew themselves; and in which they were reconciled by God beyond any reconciliation they could offer one another.

The Christian faith has no good news in it unless the Bible is true: unless it is both God's book and ours, uncoerced human testimony and unconditional divine grace; unless the initiative experienced and witnessed to by the Bible's human authors and their fellows—persons not unlike ourselves—really happened, and happens still wherever men and women, touched and made expectant by that witness, are willing to let God be God.

SIN AND SALVATION

The Christian message is about sin and salvation. Fundamentalists have continued to talk doggedly about sin and salvation at a time in cultural history when it is more fashionable to talk about the problem of emotional dysfunction and the need for therapy. For that focus they deserve the gratitude of nonfundamentalists. The most available language Americans have for talking about the nature of the human predicament they borrow from the psychotherapeutic establishment, fundamentalist efforts to the contrary notwithstanding; and establishment psychotherapy discourages talk about sin and salvation, when it does not actually repudiate it. Some years ago, O. Hobart Mowrer, then professor of psychology at the University of Illinois, and somewhat later Dr. Karl Menninger, of the Kansas clinic that bears his name, attempted to reinstate sin in the authorized vocabulary of psychotherapy; they were either treated as cultural throwbacks or cordially ignored. That may explain, and not just incidentally, why psychotherapy is so frequently inconclusive: it refuses to acknowledge or address what is, in fact, the central human problem.

Fundamentalism itself is responsible for some of this popular repudiation of sin because it ties its doctrine of sin to simpleminded interpretations of Eden as a place to be located on a map, of Adam and Eve as our literal first progenitors, and of sin as the universal racial inheritance resulting from their primal misdeed. Of course that is nonsense! But sin is an "original" fact about us. Our own natures as centered selves is a sufficient explanation for our sometimes subtle, sometimes savage attempts to remake the world in our own image.

If I understand that ancient doctrine of original sin rightly, it says that all my life long I—and every other woman and man with me—struggle with, and regularly succumb to, the temptation to treat the universe as if its center were located precisely at the place where I stand, and not elsewhere; as if its topography were drawn to the contours I see, and not otherwise; and as if its horizons were exactly where I measure them, no nearer, no farther. Who can deny the accuracy of that description for his, for her, own life?

Fundamentalism has sometimes tied its doctrine of sin to outrageous notions of "total depravity," as if all of our efforts are directly contrary to the good, the true, and the beautiful. Of course that is nonsense too! The doctrine of original sin does not deny that we achieve much that is good; rather it insists that even the best we do is touched and tainted by our self-interestedness. It does not deny that we may possess truth, even truth about the absolute; rather, it refutes our claim to possess absolute truth. It does not deny our discrimination of beauty; rather, it warns against our eagerness to profit from ugliness. It does not deny our capacity to love; rather, it discloses our readiness to idolize.

Sin is broken love, fallen love. Says Jean-Baptiste Clamence in Albert Camus's novel *The Fall*, "It is not true that I never loved. I conceived at least one great love in my life, of which I was always the object." Salvation is our restoration to the love for which Love has made us. Salvation means salving, healing; and healing is wholing, the overcoming of brokenness. Christ himself is held, in the New Testament, to be the whole man, humanhood completed, the New Adam. When Christian doctrine speaks of the sinlessness of Christ, it means that his was not a broken, fallen love. And when we experience the accepting and reconciling love of God in Jesus as the Christ, we are enabled, at least here and there, now and then, to love as he loved, and in those moments to experience our own wholeness—our healing, our salving.

If we are grateful for fundamentalist persistence in pressing the centrality of sin and salvation in the Christian faith, we may nevertheless regret that, in fundamentalist hands, being "saved" or "born again" is so often seized as a mark of spiritual and moral superiority over the "unsaved," that is, those—whether nonfundamentalist Christians or non-Christians—whose experience differs from that of fundamentalists. Indeed, for some fundamentalists, being "saved" confers legitimacy on the use of the most violent and unloving rhetoric in denouncing and damning the "unsaved" and on taking delight in contemplating the destruction that is presumed to await them in the providence of an irreconcilable fundamentalist God. By gospel standards, that is broken, fallen love, unmitigated by any saving grace, and it is far from what the New Testament calls us to. If Jesus' teaching means anything, it means that we are simply not permitted to divide the world into those who are "our kind" and those who are "not our kind," with permission to will the good of the former and to depreciate and despise the latter. Rather, the love to which faith in Christ restores us broadens the range of our kinship and caring rather than narrowing it, making even the enemy our sister and brother. Rather than conferring upon us a superiority, the salving of Christ-like love makes it possible to see ourselves and others in proper proportion for the first time. Blaise Pascal described the loving and therefore proportioned attitude believers ought to take toward unbelievers, in words fundamentalists would do well to hear and heed: "Our religion obliges us always to consider them, so long as they are alive, capable of being illuminated by grace, and to believe that in a short while they may be fuller of faith than we ourselves, while we, on the other hand, may fall into the blindness that is now theirs."

THE NEED FOR DECISION

The Christian message demands a decision. It is not incidental that the series of radio programs sponsored by the Billy Graham Evangelistic Association was called "The Hour of Decision." Every sermon Graham preaches—and in this he resembles every other evangelist—drives toward an appeal for a decision on the part of his hearers, usually the decision to accept Jesus Christ as Lord and Savior, whether for the first time or as a recommitment. Christians from mainline Protestant churches are likely to be uncomfortable when Graham's service arrives at the moment of invitation. That discomfort arises partly because the evangelist's appeal seems much too simple. Giving one's heart to Jesus is an enormously serious matter, with transformative implications that reach into every aspect of one's life and relationships. The evangelist has scarcely touched upon those implications in the course of his homiletical appeal, nor could he conceivably do so within its limits; and one suspects that the "prayer counselors," who work briefly with those who come forward in response to the appeal for decision, have neither the time nor the competence to help trace the consequences that may flow from the deceptively simple act of coming forward, if it is taken with full seriousness.

The discomfort arises, as well, out of the fact that mainline Christians are seldom, if ever, confronted by a demand for decision in the services conducted in their own churches. The central issues of Christian belief may be conscientiously addressed there, and the imperatives of a Christian ethical life may be thoughtfully and persuasively presented—issues of feeding the hungry and sheltering the homeless, of racial and gender equity, of war and peace. But the women and men who sit in those services, and who Sunday after Sunday are urged to faith and practice, are not presented then and there with an invitation to take a public stand before God and in the face of that congregation, committing themselves either to deepen their faith or to the specific practice of it.

They are not directly invited because, for the most part, mainline clergy do not ascribe to themselves—perhaps better, do not arrogate to themselves—the authoritarian posture commonly adopted by evangelists, who are quite ready to tell people precisely what they ought to believe and, more and more these days, how they ought to think and vote on public issues. Not that the mainline preachers lack doctrinal or political conviction themselves; but they are likely to think that they would expropriate the work of the Holy Spirit if they were to go beyond making issues of faith, the options for belief, utterly clear by trying in effect to demand assent from their hearers. After all, Paul in 1 Corinthians 12:3 asserted that "no one can say 'Jesus is Lord' except by the Holy Spirit." So preaching and witness can be, at best, preparation for a decision in the lives of individual men and women that will be the work of that Spirit, rather than a psychologically coercive substitute for that work.

There is another factor that makes us uneasy in the presence of the evangelist's invitation, this factor more existential than theological. It is the uneasiness that demand for decision always awakens in us. Decision is exclusive: when I decide for one thing, I exclude a host of other possibilities, and I cannot make any important decision without some anticipatory mourning for that loss. Decision always draws us into the presence of uncertainty. We cannot see the end from the moment of beginning; we can scarcely begin to imagine into what unexplored territory it may take us. So decision threatens and momentarily unbalances us.

The fact is, of course, that it is in commitment—decision—that we find genuine freedom, and it is in avoidance of commitment—indecision—that we are perpetually bound in the frustration of random living. Mainline churches particularly have need to raise the level of their consciousness of that existential fact. They need to find ways to institutionalize what the evangelists know about human nature without the trappings of authority and psychology that accompany it in evangelistic meetings: namely, the universal need men and women have for recurring moments of concrete, public, ritualized, and supported decision making, if the point and purpose of their existence is to be sharpened and their lives energized and empowered.

Nor is this a need only individuals have. It has been said of one mainline denomination, which I forbear to name, that it has set its doctrinal fences so widely that the sheep on the inside are indistinguishable from the goats on the outside. After the best that can be said for the virtues of a Christian inclusiveness, there is yet one more thing to be said. If congregations are unable to make institution-wide doctrinal and ethical affirmations, then they have an especially urgent need to provide individuals and groups within their memberships with recurring opportunities for concrete, public, ritualized, and socially supported commitments, if the churches themselves are to be any more than the nondescript leading the nondescript or, in Norman Cousins's telling phrase, "the bland leading the bland."

In any event, John Mason Brown was right when he said that the bystander—the indecisive one—is never innocent, as we ought to have known from the Good Samaritan parable. Jesus did say, "Follow me!" however inconveniently that may lay upon us a choice. And more pointedly still, "He who is not with me is against me, and he who does not gather with me scatters."

RELIGION'S PLACE IN THE SCHOOLS

Religion is inseparable from culture, and therefore the study of religion belongs in the curriculum of the public schools. If we must reject fundamentalism's divisive effort to insert Christian prayer into the pluralistic American classroom, and its impious notion that if we do not thus formally acknowledge God's presence there, the poor rejected deity will be powerless to gain entrance, we can nevertheless be grateful for fundamentalism's insistence that if religion is ignored in public education, students will be deprived of an intelligent understanding of one of the driving and shaping forces in all human cultures.

Nonfundamentalists have a stake in fundamentalism's effort to win recognition for the fact that secularism is not neutral as distinct from religious options but is itself a belief system; it is precisely one of the religious options, and therefore it should not be treated preferentially in the public school curriculum. The fact is that secularism is treated preferentially. Public schools commonly reject the teaching of so-called creation science, which accounts for the origin of the universe and of humankind in terms that are compatible with the book of Genesis, because it is not really science but religion and would give preference to the view of one particular religious party, namely Christian fundamentalism. Instead, the schools teach an account of the origin of things that excludes any religious interpretation of creation whatever. This is not neutral teaching with respect to religion, as they may allege; rather, failure to include religious significance in such teaching is to teach that religion has no significance.

Writers and publishers of textbooks on American history have systematically excluded information about religious motivations, for example, in the founding of this country, in the campaign against slavery, in the civil rights struggle, and in the opposition to the Vietnam War. One book on world history omits all mention of the Reformation. A textbook that lists 300 important events in American history includes only 3 related to religion, the last of which was in 1775. Another with a list of 450 important events also includes only three related to religion: the Pilgrim landing of 1620, the Maryland Toleration Act of 1649, and the Mormon founding of Salt Lake City in 1847. One text, in discussing the issue of "manifest destiny," ascribed that view to people in the 1840s who "felt it was the clear fate of the United States to expand all the way to the Pacific." In fact, "manifest destiny" was the notion that God had expressly chosen this country for a mission to dominate the world with Anglo-Saxon Christian culture.

People of the American Way, in a published analysis of textbook content, said:

> While history textbooks talk about the existence of religious diversity in America, they do not show it: Jews exist only as the objects of discrimination; Catholics exist to be discriminated against and to ask for government money for their own schools; there is no reflection of the diversity of American Protestantism . . . ; the Quakers are shown giving us religious freedom and abolition, and then they apparently disappear off the face of the earth.[3]

The result of such so-called education is twofold: students leave school with the most appalling absence of understanding, and indeed with misunderstanding, of the nature and influence of religion, and they acquire an assumption that secular interpretations and influences have predominated in the shaping of American and other cultures.

If nonfundamentalists can make common cause with fundamentalists in seeking to alter this disastrous state of educational affairs, nonfundamentalists will depart from fundamentalists in advocating a remedy for the situation. The religious right has been actively seeking control of local school boards in order to eliminate any curricular materials that are antithetical to fundamentalist views and to insert materials that inculcate fundamentalist understandings. That policy merely substitutes one kind of religious preference for another and continues the subversion of the pluralistic society intended for this nation in its founding.

Nonfundamentalists will not urge that all favorable references to secularism be abolished but that the curriculum should include a fair statement of all of the major religious traditions and value systems and a proportioned account of their influence on the shaping of the American experience. A similar account should be offered of religious influences in other major cultures around the world, in order to free students from ethnocentric limitations and permit them to live understandingly amid the world's pluralism.

RELIGION'S PLACE IN POLITICS

Politics has need of religious influence. If we must reject the fundamentalists' effort to turn the political process into a contest between the clearly delineated forces of Christ and those of Anti-Christ—clearly delineated by their own definition, of course—we can nevertheless be grateful for fundamentalism's recent conversion to the view that politics cannot be separated from religious insight without losing its moral moorings and the vision of its larger and longer human and humane purposes.

However much we may or may not be attracted to individual candidates for the presidency who are ordained clergymen, or to presidents, like Jimmy Carter and Ronald Reagan, who give public expression to their religious convictions, we ought to be alarmed by the view, widely influential among us, that there is an incompatibility between serious religious commitment and qualification for public office. In John Kennedy's campaign, the public wanted assurance that his Roman Catholicism would not determine his actions as president; and more recently, assurances were extracted from Supreme Court nominee Anthony Kennedy that his religion—again, Roman Catholic—would not influence his decisions on the high court.

This view appears to come from two sources. One is the religious right that still harbors its traditional prejudice against Catholicism, viewing it as subversive in doctrine and superstitious in practice. In the case of the right, the problem is not the incompatibility of religious commitment and public office, so long as that commitment is fundamentalist; it is, simply, a distrust of committed nonfundamentalists in office.

The other source is that enclave on the left that views politics as an amoral process at best, where prudent considerations are about as lofty as the ethics of public office can be permitted to get, and where pragmatism and accommodation are the requisite talents ("Go along to get along," is the classic statement given to this view by one eminent speaker of the House). Under these conditions, public officials who have a strong moral sense rooted in serious religious conviction are seen as irrelevant to political debate or as dangerous to it because of their ability to distract the public-policy process with their irrelevancies and to stall the machinery of compromise.

Of course, this view of the political process is not non-ideological, as its proponents may pretend, but reflects an ideology of its own, with secular commitments no less "religious" in their own way than those of conventional Christians and Jews because they are rooted in a systematic secular worldview. So, like its clones on the religious right, the problem for the secular left is not really the incompatibility of serious ideological commitment to public office, so long as that commitment is to the secular ideology; it is, rather, a distrust of committed nonsecularists in office.

The historian Christopher Lasch has found, in my view at least, the richly suggestive beginning of a response to both the right and the left in this critically important matter:

> The proper reply to right-wing religiosity is not to insist that "politics and religion don't mix." This is the stock response of the left, which has been caught off guard by the revival of religious concerns and by the insistence—by no means confined to the religious right—that politics without religion is no politics at all. Bewildered by the sudden interest in "social issues," the left would like either to get them off the political agenda or, failing that, to redefine them as economic issues. . . .
>
> The problem isn't how to keep religion out of politics but how to subject political life to spiritual criticism without

losing sight of the tension between the political and the spiritual realm. . . . A complete separation of religion and politics, whether it arises out of religious indifference or out of its opposite, . . . religious passion . . . , condemns the political realm to "perpetual warfare," as Niebuhr argued in *Moral Man and Immoral Society*. . . . The only way to break the cycle is to subject oneself and one's political friends to the same rigorous moral standards to which one subjects one's opponents and to invoke spiritual standards, moreover, not merely to condemn one's opponents but also to understand and forgive them. . . . [We need] a politics of "angerless wisdom," a politics of nonviolent coercion that seeks to resolve the endless argument about means and ends by making nonviolent means, openness, and truth-telling political ends in their own right.[4]

LANGUAGE AND HUMANNESS

Language is "the defining mystery" of our humanness. It is our capacity for the word that makes each of us human and marks us off from the dumb world around us. The literary critic George Steiner has put the point with near poetic force, in writing that "language is the defining mystery of man. . . . in it his identity and historical presence are uniquely explicit. It is language that severs man from the signal codes, from the inarticulacies, from the silences that inhabit the greater part of being." The apostle Paul seemed to understand that when, in Romans, he wrote:

> "For everyone who calls upon the name of the Lord will be saved." But how are men to call upon him in whom they have not believed? And how are they to believe in him of whom they have never heard? And how are they to hear without a preacher?" . . . So faith comes from what is heard, and what is heard comes by the preaching of Christ.[5]

Whatever else resurgent fundamentalism may be, I believe it is at least in part a judgment against the mainstream American pulpit, which has failed to give men and women the clear and convincing faith-language they need to get on with their lives. *Habits of the Heart*, that important inquiry into the American character, researched and written by

Robert Bellah and his associates, has told us unequivocally that Americans today lack a language that is needed to make moral sense of their lives, with the result that there is an enormous amount of confusion both about personal relationships and about social goods. We lack, say its authors, "a language to explain what seem to be the real commitments that define [our] lives, and to that extent the commitments themselves are precarious." Their research found that the most widespread language used by Americans comes out of the "therapeutic culture"; but that is the language they call "expressive individualism," which urges each person to fashion his or her own private meaning and which, as a consequence, leaves the individual "suspended [in] terrifying isolation." The message of those social-science researchers is that "it is a powerful cultural fiction that we not only can, but must, make up our deepest beliefs in the isolation of our private lives," and that the crisis in the American character springs precisely from that fiction.

What has happened in American society to cause thousands of men and women to seek meaning in the privatized process of psychotherapy and priestly ministration from the psychotherapist, and has sent thousands of others to fundamentalist evangelists for guidance in meaning and morals? Harsh as it may sound, I believe that part of the responsibility for those developments can be traced to a rhetorical and spiritual void that we have permitted to invade the pulpits of mainstream Protestantism.

A great deal is being written and said, these days, about achieving a new vitality for the churches through the techniques of congregational growth and development, on the one hand, and the discipline of spirituality, on the other. And there is no doubt that much good can come from improving organizational process and outreach and from cultivating deeper habits of contemplation. One gains the impression, however—at least by omission—that it is possible to achieve these outward and inward dimensions of renewal without reference to the pulpit, casting the minister in the skilled role of corporate leader or of spiritual director, with scant attention to preaching.

I want to suggest another route to the outward and inward vivification of the churches, one that springs from a Renaissance-like and, as I believe, biblical awareness of the renewing potency of the word. Renaissance man, says A. Bartlett Giamatti, understood the transformative power of language.

> Words were units of energy. Through words man could assume forms and aspire to shapes and states otherwise beyond his reach. Words had this immense potency, this virtue, because they were derived from and were images of the Word, the Word of God which made us and which was God. Used properly, words could shape us in His image, and lead us to salvation. Through praise, in its largest sense, our words approach their source in the Word, and, therefore, we approach Him.[6]

If mainstream churches are to have anything to give to the unchurched and the dechurched whom churches seek to draw by the techniques of congregational development and outreach, or to have any effect on the superficial spirituality of many of the churched, there must be a historical and figurative renaissance of the pulpit—a recovery of what the first and sixteenth centuries knew, and of what fundamentalist evangelists, to their credit, seem to understand: that "faith comes by hearing, and what is heard comes by the preaching of Christ."

Key Terms

Apocalypse, apocalyptic—literally, a revealing of what is hidden. The terms refer to a time of cosmic judgment, in which the evil ruling powers of this world will be destroyed and God's faithful will be vindicated and returned to their proper status in the divine order of things. Apocalyptic literature was written in order to encourage faithfulness until the time of vindication, which, though presently hidden from view, was surely coming. That literature, depicting the judgment and vindication, emerged primarily out of the second and first centuries B.C. and the first century A.D., times of persecution for Jews and for Christians. Since the prophetic period was long past and there were no prophets present in the land to declare God's righteousness and judgment against evil, the authors of this literature used pseudonyms in their writing, attributing it to some ancient worthy as a means of adding to its spiritual authority. Apocalyptic writing utilizes symbol and image—the contents of dreams and visions—whose hidden meaning requires interpretation; hence, again, the literal meaning of the term. Apocalyptic literature in the Old Testament consists chiefly of the books of Ezekiel and Daniel, and in the New Testament of Matthew 24–25, Mark 13, and Revelation (which was originally called the Apocalypse of John). Many other apocalpytic writings were produced but are not recognized in the standard Hebrew-Christian canon, including Enoch, Jubilees, the Assumption of Moses, the Testaments of the Patriarchs, the Apocalypse of Ezra, the Apocalypse of Baruch, and the Sibylline Oracles.

Atavism—the reappearance in an individual of characteristics of some remote ancestor that have been absent in intervening generations; reversion to an earlier type.

Carapace—"an attitude or state of mind . . . serving to promote or isolate from external influence," says *Webster's New Collegiate Dictionary*. The term is used by Martin Marty to describe the nature of fundamentalism's relation to the wider culture of modernism.

Conservative—in this book, primarily a reference to those Christians who share many doctrinal convictions with both fundamentalists and evangelicals (e.g., the deity of Christ, Christ's atoning death on the cross), doing so with a high view of the inspiration and authority of the scripture but without the additional baggage either of "inerrancy" or "infallibility." Like evangelicals, conservative Christians take a moderate, ecumenical approach to other Christians who do not share their doctrinal views in detail.

Evangelical—in this book, primarily a reference to those Christians who share many of the doctrinal convictions of both fundamentalists and conservatives, while repudiating biblical "inerrancy" in favor of "infallibility," which affirms the absolute reliability of the Bible's saving truth without being obliged to defend the total accuracy of its secular knowledge. Most evangelicals have come out of fundamentalism and have rejected its behavioral and rhetorical extremism in favor of a more irenic style, permitting them to admit the possibility of incompleteness in their own views and to entertain the partial rightness of views that may differ from theirs in the main, whether on their theological left or right.

Evangelicalism—used exclusively in this book to designate the movement of spiritual awakening in America that began in the 1720s and continued more or less up to the Civil War. The chief vehicle of the movement was the religious revival meeting, and the message of the revivalists was commonly marked by a proclamation of the love of Christ and, in that light, an emphasis on the need for both individual and social reform, an essential optimism about human nature and history, and a call to missionary activity. During the era of evangelicalism, more new educational institutions were founded than in any other period of American history. Evangelicalism is the common spiritual heritage, and the common historical point of divergence, for the later development of the major religious groups—conservatives, liberals, fundamentalists, and evangelicals—in the present era of American Protestantism.

Fundamentalist—in this book, primarily a reference to those Christians who believe in the total errorlessness—inerrancy—of the Bible in all of its assertions, of whatever kind; who believe that the present, penultimate dispensation of history will end in utter disaster, as have all of its predecessors; who expect the imminent, public return of Christ in a second advent that will usher in the final dispensation of history; and who feel bound by faithfulness to an inerrant scripture to anathematize, and to separate themselves from, those who take a different view, whether they be Christians or others.

Incarnation—the full and unmodified subsistence of both the divine and the human natures in Jesus as the Christ; i.e., God fully present under the conditions of history. The central affirmation of Christian orthodoxy, this doctrine is also its central mystery, miracle, and paradox: how is it possible for both natures to be fully present under the conditions of history? Orthodox Christians, persuaded that they have experienced for themselves the truth of this mystery, believe that it is enough to confess that truth, preparing others to experience it as well, without feeling obliged to demonstrate it by rational argument. The late Archibishop of Canterbury William Temple once said that anyone who says he can explain the meaning of the incarnation simply demonstrates that he does not understand its meaning.

Liberalism, modernism, new theology—in this book, terms that all refer to the same effort to reconcile and adapt Christian faith and life to nineteenth- and twentieth-century knowledge and experience. In a more analytical study, it is possible to make useful distinctions, for example, between liberalism and modernism (see my *American Theology in the Liberal Tradition*, chapter 4).

Millennialism—the expectation of the thousand-year reign of Christ. The **millennium** is, literally, a period of a thousand years. It follows the *Tribulation* (see below) and precedes the final judgment of Satan and his minions and the coming of "a new heaven and a new earth." The millennium is expected to be a time of unparalleled peace and prosperity. Millennialism refers, in current use, to the expectation that Christ will return to earth in a second advent. **Premillennialists** believe that, since the world is irreformable, historical progress being an illusion, Christ must return in order to redeem the world's present misery and evil and, by transforming history, usher in the thousand-year-long golden age. **Postmillennialists,** who were revivalists prior to the Civil War, held that God is actively at work within history to bring about increasing progress toward spiritual and material beatitude, and that Christ will return after the golden age has been established. Later liberals perpetuated this view of historical progress but detached it from an expectation of Christ's literal return.

Neo-orthodoxy—a twentieth-century theological movement that is both an heir of liberalism and its most telling critic. Accepting certain features of the liberal view—e.g., a historical and critical reading of the Bible, a positive attitude toward modern scientific inquiry, insistence on the social relevance of the Christian message—neo-orthodox theologians nevertheless chastised the liberals for their inadequate understanding of tragedy and sin and of the transcendence of God; for their neglect of the doctrine of the church; and for their relatively uncritical identification of religion with secular culture. Neo-orthodoxy is identified in the United States with the work of Reinhold Niebuhr and his followers, and in Europe with the work of Karl Barth and the Barthians, though there are significant differences between the two schools. Neo-orthodox theologians drew much of their theological corrective from the Reformation, especially from Martin Luther and John Calvin, and from early church fathers, such as Augustine of Hippo, and medieval theologians, such as Anselm of Canterbury.

Orthodoxy—for Protestants, a theological tradition shaped by the sixteenth-century reformers, especially Martin Luther and John Calvin. They, in turn, recovered the work of earlier theologians (Augustine of Hippo is a prime example for both reformers; Luther was, in fact, a monk of the Augustianian order) and reappropriated the formulations of early ecumenical councils (e.g., the Council of Nicaea (325) and the Council of Chalcedon (451). All of these resources were utilized by the reformers in that reinterpretation of scripture that became the ground for their controversy with the Roman Catholic Church, and for the fashioning of the central stream of Protestant thought throughout the centuries since. The Lutheran branch of orthodoxy was captured in the Augsburg Confession of 1531, the Reformed (with Calvin as its primary source) in the Westminster Confession of 1647.

Pentecostals—whether formally (by denominational affiliation) or informally (by practice), Christians who believe that the Holy Spirit continues to descend upon men and women, giving them the gifts of special utterance, as was first given to the Apostles on the day of Pentecost (see Acts 2). "Speaking in tongues" is sometimes unintelligible, a sign of the Holy Spirit's mysterious presence and power in the speaker, and sometimes intelligible, moving the speaker to prophesy and to interpret the mysteries of God. Pentecostals also believe in God-initiated visions and conversations and that the immediate indwelling of the Holy Spirit confers upon them the power to cast out demons, to heal, and to perform other miracles in Christ's name, including even the raising of the dead.

The apostle Paul has some things, positively and negatively, to say about speaking in tongues in 1 Corinthians 12:1–11, 13:1–3; and 14:1–19. *Biblicist* fundamentalists believe that legitimate speaking in tongues ceased at the end of the apostolic period, God having given us the gift of scripture as his own Word and our all-sufficient guide. They believe that in its contemporary expression, speaking in tongues is an effort of the Devil to confuse and traduce the faithful and that it undermines the authority of scripture as the sole source of Christian truth. The largest Pentecostal denomination is the Assemblies of God, from which Jim Bakker and Jimmy Swaggart derived their ordination. Pat Robertson (Baptist) and Oral Roberts (Methodist) are Pentecostals, not in denomination but in the practice of speaking in tongues, conversing with God, healing, and other miraculous interventions.

Rapture—a term not found in the New Testament but adopted by fundamentalists to designate what will happen to the faithful at the time of Christ's return to earth. Those who have died in the faith, and those who are still alive at the time of his coming, "shall be caught up together . . . in the clouds to meet the Lord in the air" [1 Thessalonians 4:16–18]. Fundamentalists are not all agreed on when the Rapture will occur, whether at the beginning of the **Tribulation** (see below), thus rescuing true Christians from the terrible time; in its midst; or at its end, requiring Christians to pass through that time of testing. Neither are fundamentalists agreed on whether or not the Rapture and the second coming are synonymous. Some believe that they are the same event; others, like Hal Lindsey, believe in a "secret Rapture," when the living faithful will be spirited away at the beginning of the Tribulation—they will simply disappear from their normal walks of life—to be with Christ until the Tribulation is over. Then the public second coming of Christ will occur ("every eye shall see him," [Revelation 1:7]), and at that time those who have already died in the faith will be raised to be with Christ, along with those who were joined to him in the "secret Rapture" rescue mission. Lindsey calls the Rapture "the ultimate trip."

Revelation—the self-disclosure of God's character and will to humankind. All persons are marked by a certain hiddenness, so that despite our public observations of them and the clues to their character that we may draw from those observations, we do not really know who they are until they tell us their story, until they choose to reveal to us their true nature and intent. Christian theology holds that there is in God, the transcendent Person, an even more profound hiddenness; and that we cannot know the nature of that transcendence—of its intent toward us, whether friendly or hostile—until it chooses to open itself to our understanding. Most Christians affirm that the revelation of God's character has occurred, not exclusively but most authoritatively, in the mighty acts of God recorded in the Hebrew-Christian scriptures (God's story) and preeminently in the person and work of Jesus as the Christ.

Tribulation—a terrible time of testing that will occur, fundamentalists believe, at the end of the present division, or dispensation, of history as a prelude to the **millennium** (see above). That time will be marked by unprecedented natural and human disasters, the deserved outcome of the faithlessness and rebellion of humankind against God that has occurred in the historical period that precedes it. Although few fundamentalists are prepared to predict the date of its occurrence, it is expected to occur in the present era—"we are in the general time" of its coming, Hal Lindsey has said. Fundamentalists differ in their views of the relationship between the Tribulation and Christ's return to earth (see *Rapture*, above).

Trine immersion—a form of baptism. Baptism is the formal rite of admission to the Christian life and to membership in a Christian church. Although there are, in practice, a variety of modes of baptism throughout Christendom (sprinkling or pouring water on the head of the candidate being two), there is little disagreement that New Testament baptism was by full immersion of the baptismal candidate. In trine immersion, the candidate is immersed three times, once in the name of each of the three Persons of the Trinity. In many churches, baptism by water, in whatever mode, is the sole prerequisite for admission to the Lord's Supper (or eucharist). These churches are said to practice "open communion." Some churches apply other restrictions on participation in the communion rite: for example, admitting only those who have been immersed, only those who have been baptized by trine immersion, only those who have been baptized in a church of the same denomination as the observing church, or even only those who have been baptized in the very local church in which the communion is to be observed. Such churches are said to practice "closed communion."

Sources and Suggested Reading

I gladly acknowledge my debt to the following sources of primary and secondary material upon which I have depended for information and insight. The works cited will also serve admirably as suggestions for further reading.

Chapter 1
Arnall, Ellis G. *The Shore Dimly Seen*. Philadelphia: Lippincott, 1946.
Averill, Lloyd J. *The Problem of Being Human*. Valley Forge, Pa.: Judson Press, 1974.
Butterfield, Herbert. *Christianity and History*. New York: Charles Scribner's Sons, 1950.

Chapter 2
Averill, Lloyd J. *American Theology in the Liberal Tradition*. Philadelphia: Westminster Press, 1967.
Carnell, Edward J. "Fundamentalism." In *A Handbook of Christian Theology*, ed. Marvin Halverson and Arthur A. Cohen. New York: Meridian Books, 1958.
Falwell, Jerry, with Ed Dobson and Ed Hindson. *The Fundamentalist Phenomenon: The Resurgence of Conservative Christianity*. Garden City, N.Y.: Doubleday & Co., 1981.
Gaillard, Frye. "The Political Education of Billy Graham," *The Washington Post National Weekly Edition* (14 April 1986).
Hutchison, William R., ed. *American Protestant Thought: The Liberal Era*. New York: Harper & Row, 1968.

Machen, J. Gresham. *Christianity and Liberalism.* Grand Rapids, Mich.: Eerdmans, 1923.

Marsden, George. *Fundamentalism and American Culture: The Shaping of Twentieth-Century Evangelicalism 1870–1925.* New York: Oxford University Press, 1980.

Marty, Martin E. *Modern American Religion.* Vol. 1, *The Irony of It All 1893–1919.* Chicago: University of Chicago Press, 1986.

Morgan, Dan. "Blest Be the Tie that Binds—If It Exists at All." *The Washington Post National Weekly Edition* (13 April 1987).

Niebuhr, H. Richard. *The Kingdom of God in America.* Hamden, Conn.: Shoestring Press, 1956.

Russell, C. Allyn. *Voices of American Fundamentalism: Seven Biographical Studies.* Philadelphia: Westminster Press, 1976.

Sandeen, Ernest R. *The Roots of Fundamentalism: British and American Millenarianism 1800–1930.* Chicago: University of Chicago Press, 1970.

Scofield, C.I., and others. *The Scofield Reference Bible.* New York: Oxford University Press, 1917.

Sider, Ronald J. "A Plea for Conservative Radicals and Radical Conservatives." *The Christian Century* (10 October 1986).

Chapter 3

Althaus, Paul. *The Theology of Martin Luther,* trans. by Robert C. Schultz. Philadelphia: Fortress Press, 1966.

Averill, Lloyd J. *Between Faith and Unfaith.* Atlanta: John Knox Press, 1968.

Butterfield, Herbert. *Christianity and History.* New York: Charles Scribner's Sons, 1950.

Carnell, Edward J. *An Introduction to Christian Apologetics.* Grand Rapids, Mich.: Eerdmans, 1948.

Dayton, Donald B. "'The Battle for the Bible': Renewing the Inerrancy Debate." *The Christian Century* (10 November 1976).

Falwell, Jerry, with Ed Dobson and Ed Hindson. *The Fundamentalist Phenomenon: The Resurgence of Conservative Christianity.* Garden City, N.Y.: Doubleday & Co., 1981.

Henry, Carl F.H., ed. *Contemporary Evangelical Thought.* Great Neck, N.Y.: Channel Press, 1957.

Lindsell, Harold, and Charles J. Woodbridge. *A Handbook of Christian Truth.* Old Tappan, N.J.: Fleming H. Revell Co., 1953.

Marsden, George. *Reforming Fundamentalism: Fuller Seminary and the New Evangelicalism.* Grand Rapids, Mich.: Eerdmans, 1987.

McKim, Donald K. *What Christians Believe About the Bible.* New York: Thomas Nelson, 1985.

Montgomery, John Warwick, ed. *God's Inerrant Word: An Inter-*

national Symposium on the Trustworthiness *of Scripture*. Bethany Fellowship, 1974.

Niesel, Wilhelm. *The Theology of John Calvin*, trans. by Harold McKnight. Philadelphia: Westminster Press, n.d..

Seeberg, Reinhold. *Textbook of the History of Doctrines*. Vol. 2, *The History of Doctrines in the Middle and Early Modern Ages*. Grand Rapids, Mich.: Baker Book House, 1952.

Young, Edward J. *Thy Word Is Truth: Some Thoughts on the Biblical Doctrine of Inspiration*. Grand Rapids, Mich.: Eerdmans, 1957.

Chapter 4

Averill, Lloyd J. *The Problem of Being Human*. Valley Forge, Pa.: Judson Press, 1974.

Bell, Terrel H. *The Thirteenth Man: A Reagan Cabinet Memoir*. New York: Free Press, 1988.

Blumenthal, Sidney. "An Attitude Not an Agenda." *The Washington Post National Weekly Edition* (14 October 1985).

Blumhofer, Edith L. "Divided Pentecostals: Bakker vs. Swaggart." *The Christian Century* (6 May 1986).

Brinton, Crane. *The Shaping of the Modern Mind*. New York: New American Library, 1953.

Carnell, Edward J. "Fundamentalism." In *A Handbook of Christian Theology*, ed. Marvin Halverson and Arthur A. Cohen. New York: Meridian Books, 1958.

Falwell, Jerry. *Listen, America!* Garden City, N.Y.: Doubleday & Co., 1980.

FitzGerald, Frances. *Cities on a Hill: A Journey Through Contemporary American Cultures*. New York: Simon & Schuster, 1987.

Gaillard, Frye. "The Political Education of Billy Graham." *The Washington Post National Weekly Edition* (14 April 1986).

Henry, Carl F.H. *The Uneasy Conscience of Modern Fundamentalism*. Grand Rapids, Mich.: Eerdmans, 1947.

Lasch, Christopher. "What's Wrong with the Right." *Tikkun: A Quarterly Jewish Critique of Politics, Culture & Society*, Vol. 1, No. 1.

Marty, Martin E. *Righteous Empire: The Protestant Experience in America*. New York: Dial Press, 1970.

Marty, Martin E. "A Profile of Norman Lear: Another Pilgrim's Progress." *The Christian Century* (21 January 1987).

Miller, William Lee. "The Ghost of Freedoms Past." *The Washington Post National Weekly Edition* (13 October 1986).

Sawyer, Kathy. "Fundamental Conflict on the Right." *The Washington Post National Weekly Edition* (14 January 1985).

Sontag, Frederick, and John Roth. *The American Religious Expe-*

rience: The Roots, Trends, and Future of American Theology. New York: Harper & Row, 1972.

Will, George. In a column syndicated by the Washington Post Writers Group, published in the *Seattle Post-Intelligencer* (9 November 1986).

Young, Perry Deane. *God's Bullies: Power Politics and Religious Tyranny.* New York: Holt, Rinehart & Winston, 1982.

Chapter 5

Ahlstrom, Sydney. *A Religious History of the American People.* New Haven: Yale University Press, 1972.

Armstrong, Herbert W. *The United States and British Commonwealth in Prophecy.* Pasadena, Cal.: Ambassador College Press, 1972.

Armstrong, Herbert W. *Who Is the Beast?* Pasadena, Cal.: Worldwide Church of God, 1980.

Gritsch, Eric. *Born Againism: Perspectives on a Movement.* Philadelphia: Fortress Press, 1982.

Halsell, Grace. *Prophecy and Politics: Militant Evangelists on the Road to Nuclear War.* Westport, Conn.: Lawrence Hill & Co., 1986.

Kepler, Thomas F. *Dreams of the Future.* Nashville: Abingdon Press, 1963.

LaHaye, Tim. *The Coming Peace in the Middle East.* Grand Rapids, Mich.: Zondervan, 1984.

Lindsey, Hal, with C.C. Carlson. *The Late Great Planet Earth.* New York: Bantam Books, 1973.

Martin, William. "Waiting for the End." *The Atlantic Monthly* (June 1982).

Schweitzer, Albert. *The Quest of the Historical Jesus.* New York: Macmillan, 1968.

Scofield, C.I., and others. *The Scofield Reference Bible.* New York: Oxford University Press, 1917.

White, E.G. *America in Prophecy.* Jemison, Ala.: Audio Visual Production, n.d..

Chapter 6

Bellah, Robert N., and others. *Habits of the Heart.* New York: Harper & Row, 1985.

Giamatti, A. Bartlett. *Exile and Change in Renaissance Literature.* New Haven: Yale University Press, 1983.

Lasch, Christopher. "What's Wrong with the Right." *Tikkun: A Quarterly Jewish Critique of Politics, Culture & Society,* Vol. 1, No. 1.

Menninger, Karl. *Whatever Became of Sin?* New York: Hawthorn Books, 1973.

Nord, Warren A. "Liberals Should Want Religion Taught in Public Schools." *The Washington Post National Weekly Edition* (21 July 1986).

Otto, Max. *The Human Enterprise.* New York: F.C. Crofts & Co., 1941.

Russell, Bertrand. *A History of Western Philosophy.* New York: Simon & Schuster, 1945.

Steiner, George. *Language and Silence: Essays on Language, Literature, and the Inhuman.* New York: Atheneum, 1967.

Vobejda, Barbara. "Texts Go Too Far in Ignoring Role of Church in U.S.," *The Washington Post,* reprinted in *The Seattle Times* (10 May 1987).

Notes

Chapter 1

1. The Rubáiyát of Omar Khayyám, Rendered into English Verse by Edward Fitzgerald, 1st ed. 1859 (Portland, Me.: Thomas B. Mosher, 1900), Quatrain LI, p. 54.

2. Ellis Arnall, The Shore Dimly Seen (Philadelphia: J.B. Lippincott, 1946), p. 128.

3. Herbert Butterfield, Christianity and History (New York: Charles Scribner's Sons, 1950), p. 146.

Chapter 2

1. Newman Smyth, Old Faiths in New Light (New York: Charles Scribner's Sons, 1879). Quoted in John Wright Buckham, Progressive Religious Thought in America (New York: Houghton Mifflin, 1919), p. 268.

2. J. Gresham Machen, Christianity and Liberalism (Grand Rapids, Mich.: W.B. Eerdmans, 1923), pp. 7, 173.

3. A.A. Hodge and Benjamin B. Warfield, "Inspiration," in The Presbyterian Review, 2 (April, 1881), quoted in George Marsden, Fundamentalism and American Culture (New York: Oxford University Press, 1980), p. 113.

4. Curtis Lee Laws, in The Watchman-Examiner (July 1, 1920), quoted in Context 19, No. 7 (April 1, 1987).

5. Luke 4:18–19.

6. Alexander Carson, The Inspiration of Scripture (1830), quoted in Ernest R. Sandeen, The Roots of Fundamentalism (Chicago: University of Chicago Press, 1970), p. 113.

7. Westminster Confession, quoted in Ernest R. Sandeen, The Roots of Fundamentalism (Chicago: University of Chicago Press, 1970), pp. 118–119.

8. Ibid., p. 129.

9. Hodge and Warfield, "Inspiration" p. 129.

10. J. Gresham Machen, quoted in C. Allyn Russell, *Voices of American Fundamentalism* (Philadelphia: Westminster Press, 1976), p. 142.

11. John Roach Straton, quoted in Harry Emerson Fosdick, *The Living of These Days* (New York: Harper & Bros., 1950), p. 153.

12. *Western Recorder*, quoted in ibid., pp. 155–156.

13. Billy Sunday, quoted in George Marsden, *Fundamentalism and American Culture* (New York: Oxford University Press, 1980), p. 221.

14. Jerry Falwell, quoted in Frances FitzGerald, *Cities on a Hill* (New York: Simon & Schuster, 1987), p. 164.

15. Edward J. Carnell, "Fundamentalism," in *A Handbook of Christian Theology*, ed. Marvin Halverson and Arthur A. Cohen (New York: Meridian Books, 1958), p. 143.

16. Billy Graham, quoted in Frye Gaillard, "The Political Education of Billy Graham," *The Washington Post National Weekly Edition* (14 April 1986), p. 9.

17. Ibid., p. 8.

18. "A Covenant of Evangelical Inquiry," *The Christian Century* (10 October 1986), p. 837.

19. Ronald E. Sider, "A Plea for Conservative Radicals and Radical Conservatives," *The Christian Century* (10 October 1986), p. 838.

Chapter 3

1. Edward J. Young, *Thy Word Is Truth: Some Thoughts on the Biblical Doctrine of Inspiration* (Grand Rapids, Mich.: W. B. Eerdmans, 1957).

2. Quoted in Edward J. Carnell, *An Introduction to Christian Apologetics* (Grand Rapids, Mich.: W.B. Eerdmans, 1948), p. 207.

3. Carnell, *An Introduction to Christian Apologetics*, p. 200.

4. Harold Lindsell and Charles Woodbridge, *A Handbook of Christian Truth* (Westwood, N.J.: Fleming H. Revell Co., 1953), pp. 25–26.

Chapter 4

1. Jerry Falwell, *Listen, America!* (Garden City, N.Y.: Doubleday & Co., 1980); quoted in Perry Deane Young, *God's Bullies* (New York: Holt, Rinehart & Winston, 1982), pp. 311, 313.

2. Frances FitzGerald, *Cities on a Hill* (New York: Simon & Schuster, 1987), p. 170.

3. Ronald Reagan, quoted in "Excerpts from President's Speech to National Association of Evangelicals," *The New York Times* (9 March 1983), p. A18.

Martin Marty, "A Profile of Norman Lear: Another Pilgrim's ess," *The Christian Century* (21 January 1987), pp. 55, 58.

5. Robert Simonds, in a letter to members and friends of the National Association of Christian Educators, August/September, 1985.

6. Thomas Jefferson, "An Act for Establishing Religious Freedom" (1779).

7. Thomas Jefferson, quoted in Perry Deane Young, *God's Bullies* (New York: Holt, Rinehart & Winston, 1982), p. 188.

8. James Madison, quoted in ibid.

9. William Lee Miller, "The Ghost of Freedoms Past," in *The Washington Post National Weekly Edition* (13 October 1986), p. 23.

10. *The Seattle Times* (25 January 1987), p. A14.

11. James J. Kilpatrick, quoted in Young, *God's Bullies*, p. 67–68.

12. George Will, "Tennessee Ruling Puts Religion In, Learning Out, of School," *Seattle Post-Intelligencer* (9 November 1986), p. F3.

13. Ibid.

14. Jerry Falwell, quoted in FitzGerald, *Cities on a Hill*, pp. 156–157.

15. Kathy Sawyer, "Fundamental Conflict on the Right," *The Washington Post National Weekly Edition* (14 January 1985), p. 6.

16. Marc Tanenbaum, in "Letters," *Time* (23 September 1985), p. 10.

17. Christopher Lasch, "What's Wrong with the Right," *Tikkun: A Quarterly Jewish Critique of Politics, Culture & Society* 1, No. 1, 28.

Chapter 5
1. Ezekiel 5:9–13.
2. Ezekiel 1:5–11a.
3. Daniel 7:4–9.
4. Revelation 13:1–3, 11–12, 16–18.
5. Herbert W. Armstrong, *The United States and British Commonwealth in Prophecy* (Pasadena: Ambassador College Press, 1972), pp. 3–5 passim.
6. Ezekiel 37:12–14a.
7. Eric Gritsch, *Born Againism: Perspectives on a Movement* (Philadelphia: Fortress Press, 1982), pp. 26–27.
8. Ezekiel 5:9–12.

Chapter 6
1. Gerald Kennedy.
2. Max C. Otto, *The Human Enterprise* (New York: F.C. Crofts & Co., 1941), p. 342.

3. Barbara Vobejda, "Texts Go Too Far in Ignoring Role of Church in U.S.," *The Washington Post*, reprinted in *The Seattle Times* (10 May 1987), p. A17.

4. Christopher Lasch, "What's Wrong with the Right," *Tikkun: A Quarterly Jewish Critique of Politics, Culture & Society* 1, No. 1, 28–29.

5. Romans 10:13–14, 17.

6. A. Bartlett Giamatti, *Exile and Change in Renaissance Literature* (New Haven: Yale University Press, 1983), p. 103.

Index